IMAGES
of America

HOUMA

A 1936 bird's-eye view of downtown Houma shows the just-completed spire of St. Francis de Sales Catholic Church. Now the cathedral of the Houma-Thibodaux Catholic Diocese, it still graces the landscape. Directly across is the now demolished Terrebonne High School, which stood between Verret and School Streets. A closer look reveals the parish jail and the courthouse, which was demolished shortly after this photo was taken to make way for the new courthouse. The oak trees still stand in the courthouse square. The founders of the community donated the land for these buildings for public use. (Courtesy of Terrebonne Parish Consolidated Government.)

IMAGES
of America

HOUMA

Thomas Blum Cobb and Mara Currie

ARCADIA
PUBLISHING

N.H. Rightor, first mayor of the newly incorporated city of Houma, served from 1848 through 1856. As reflected in the 1860 census, the population never exceeded 429 citizens during this period. Houma was connected to the outside world by a series of waterways and the Price-Hine and Co. Stageline. The New Orleans, Opelousas, and Great Western Railroad began service from Terrebonne Station (now Schriever) on September 1, 1855. This service was the highlight of Mayor Rightor's administration and set the stage for Houma's growth. (Courtesy of Terrebonne Parish Consolidated Government.)

CONTENTS

ACKNOWLEDGMENTS

My grandfather, the late Leopold Blum, was a saver, and so was my grandmother, Amalia Lewald Blum. They raised me, so I am a saver also. They were both very civic-minded. Leopold represented the downtown section of old Houma on the city council from 1928 through 1946. This was a period of vast growth and improvement in city-provided services. It was also the period of the Great Depression and World War II. The foundation for the present government services for the people of Terrebonne Parish was achieved during this time frame. Fortunately, many photos of this period have survived and are reproduced here.

Blum played a large part in the 1934 centennial celebration. His friends became my friends. Randolph A. Bazet Sr. and his little "Red Book" from the centennial were an unending source of information and material. Bazet's cousin, Helen Wurzlow, wrote *I Dug Up Houma, Terrebonne* with Randolph's assistance. It contains a vast amount of area history. She used a lot of information from my collection, which is reproduced here. Judge Robert B. Butler was co-publisher with Easton Duval of the *Houma Courier*. Their September 1906 "Magazine Edition" proved very useful.

John B. Gordon, publisher of the *Houma Courier* newspaper, started *Courier* special history-laden editions on November 29, 1937, with "60,000 Frenchmen Can't Be Wrong." Happily, this tradition was continued by his successor, Ray F. Dill. They, along with my former boss, Ivy J. Smith, contributed more than they will ever know to this publication. Sixty thousand "thank yous" go to them!

Ray Dill encouraged former *Courier* staffer Helen Wurzlow to "dig" Terrebonne and start a weekly newspaper column to publish her findings. As more columns appeared in print, the "digs" became easier. *Courier* readers were eager to share their photos and history. It was agreed from the start that the columns would be printed in book form as a permanent history.

Special appreciation for the start-up of this project goes to Judy Chaisson Navarre, Juana Woodard, and Fay Plauche Holmgren. They, along with Terrebonne Parish Consolidated Government (TPCG) Director of Culture and Economic Development Mart Black, suggested that I answer the request for publication sought by Arcadia. Paul Guidry was invaluable in reproducing and providing the photos from the parish government collection. Much help and cooperation was given by Clifton Theriot, M.L.L.S. assistant professor and interim archivist at Nicholls State University's Ellender Memorial Library.

My friendship with Mara Currie started when we were *Houma Courier* staffers. We both left to follow other professions with printer's ink still in our blood. We were destined to work together when the opportunity arose to make this project a reality. To Tom, Mara's significant other, I offer my utmost appreciation for the many hours Mara shared with me, the "other significant other."

Much contained here comes from a collection inherited from family and friends. This includes photos and the history attached to them. They are referred to as the "Cobb collection."

Some photos appeared previously in *Terrebonne Parish Then and Now* and are reprinted with the permission of Heritage House Publishing. Many photos originated with Thelma Zelenka Kyser, her sister, Imelda Zelenka Hrubes, and their nephew, Louis G. Zelenka Jr.

Lastly, I offer my gratitude and love to my life partner, Donna, and our son, Michael, for their many months of sharing with me the creation of "our" project. Your understanding, encouragement, help, and appreciation of my desire to get this work published made it all worthwhile.

Thomas B. Cobb, Houma, Louisiana, June, 2004

INTRODUCTION

The earliest record of habitation in the Houma area by non-Native Americans is a Spanish land grant given to Joseph Hache prior to 1803. On February 28, 1823, the U.S. Senate, upon proof of habitation and cultivation prior to 1803, confirmed Hache's claim and recognized his grant.

Our story begins with the celebration of Houma's 100th birthday in 1934, a good vantage point of Houma history. A look back shows how Houma survived its humble beginning on the banks of a slow moving tributary of the Mississippi River. A look forward reveals the ground work of one of Houma's most progressive eras. This is the basis of today's city and parish growth and expansion, particularly in the offshore oil industry.

Terrebonne Parish, or the "good earth" parish, was created in 1822. Carved from neighboring Lafourche Parish, Terrebonne became the largest land area in Louisiana and, according to the *Encyclopedia Britannica*, one of the most populous rural areas in the world. However, due to recent coastal erosion, Terrebonne is now only the second-largest land area in the state. Terrebonne was home to two distinct cultures: farmers and timber men to the north and hunters, trappers, and fishermen residing along the lakes and waterways of the southern part of the parish. The northerners, who arrived mostly by way of the Mississippi River, bought large tracts of land and raised sugar cane and timber. They were slave holders and brought African-American culture into the mix. The southerners, who arrived in Louisiana mostly via the Gulf of Mexico, produced furs, seafood, and game.

Houma, centrally located at the conjuncture of six waterways, was the logical place for the cultures to come together. In 1834, Houma, the only incorporated community in the parish, became the parish seat. The Terrebonne Parish courthouse, government buildings, and other services were established in Houma on donated property.

It is almost impossible to conceive that the early settlers of the country had to depend upon horse-drawn vehicles over almost impassable roads and upon unreliable boat service. A trip of 50 miles was the event of a lifetime for many of them.

Before the New Orleans, Opelousas, and Great Western Railroad reached Lafourche Crossing on November 6, 1854, people of Houma and Terrebonne Parish traveled by team to Donaldsonville at the conjunction of Bayou La Fourche and the Mississippi River and on to their destination by boat. When the water was high in Bayou Lafourche, boats carrying passengers and freight operated between Thibodaux and New Orleans.

Shortly after the completion of the railroad to Terrebonne Station (now Schriever) on September 1, 1855, John Berger began the operation of a stage and express business along the Terrebonne Road, leaving Houma every morning at 9 a.m. and returning immediately after the arrival of the train from New Orleans about 11:30 a.m.

On June 3, 1871, Houma was assured of a railroad. Expropriation proceedings were processed against N.C. Wade to secure the necessary site for a station; rights of way had been obtained and engineers were engaged in staking the route.

The benefits derived from the construction of the railroad were incalculable. Before, shipping produce was a serious problem. By the existing means of transportation (flatboat), it required at least three days to reach New Orleans. Aside from damaging the goods, the cost of shipping a hogshead of sugar to New Orleans was $5. Freight often had to be loaded and unloaded two or three times before reaching New Orleans.

By June 10, 1871, the grading of the railroad had already commenced. The project was completed into Houma on January 8, 1872. Simultaneously, a wharf was constructed on Bayou Terrebonne at the terminus of the track to facilitate the unloading of cargoes into freight cars to be shipped to markets across the country.

Prior to the completion of the railroad into Houma, most heavy freight was transported by boat. The steamer *S.P. Archer*, owned by J.J. Shaffer & Company, was one of the first steam-propelled craft to operate exclusively in the parish of Terrebonne. It carried freight on the upper and lower Bayou Black, making connections with the railroad at Tigerville (Gibson).

Until Gray's telephone and telegraph line from Houma to Schriever was built in 1889, the town was without wire communication with the outside world. On July 13, 1898, the Ray Telephone System secured a franchise from the city council and inaugurated the first local service. The directory discloses that there were 40 patrons. After the Cumberland Telephone and Telegraph Co. secured a franchise in 1899, the Ray Telephone System ceased business.

Construction of the first water system began in 1902 and was completed in 1903. A small pump forced the water to an elevated tower and the mains were supplied by gravity pressure.

During 1923–1924, the water system was enlarged and a new light and water filtration plant was installed. The first municipally owned combination light and water plant was constructed during 1909 and was located at the site of the old pumping station on Main Street between Roussel and Barrow. The building and site were sold by the city on October 13, 1928.

The first electric current was supplied by a private concern and made its appearance around 1900. The old kerosene street lamps gradually gave way to modern methods.

Houma is home to a large number of descendants of the Acadians, known as "Cajuns." Cajuns are largely Roman Catholic, the dominant religion in Houma. However, Houmans and Terrebonians in general, are noted for their religious tolerance. This served the parish well when an influx of oil service workers began to arrive in the 1920s and 1930s. As a result of the influx, the local Presbyterian minister married many Creole Catholic belles and Protestant men, as the local Catholic priest refused to do so.

The Protestant parson's retirement in the 1950s was the cause for a large celebration chaired by respected Catholic members of the community, one of whom was the superintendent of schools at the time. "Parson" was given two sets of keys, one to a new Plymouth automobile and the other to a recently constructed, three-bedroom home and lot. These were all provided by a grateful community in recognition of the many years of service by Parson and his dutiful wife.

There are, by recent count, some 137 churches in Terrebonne Parish and 1 Jewish congregation. All the eating spots are thriving in this still-growing community. Public and private schools are near full capacity, with approximately 21,000 students in public and private halls of learning, including between 50 boys and 60 girls taking advantage of home schooling.

At the last census, there were 105,000 people living, working, and supporting the parish economy.

Like many downtown shopping areas, Houma's became practically deserted. What had not died was in the process of doing so. To the credit of the Terrebonne Parish Consolidated Government, it was recognized that a significant part of Houma history was being lost. The Houma Downtown Development Corporation was formed with the mandate to breathe new life into a dying downtown. Main Street property that was formerly an automotive service station was donated and became a park, a seafood packing warehouse became a museum, and a joint venture between the government and private sectors enabled downtown Houma to be reborn. Appreciation goes to the board of directors for their untiring efforts to make this a reality. Hopefully, this book will illustrate the importance of their work in preserving and finding new uses for downtown Houma.

One

HOUMA'S HUNDREDTH

Everything was ready for the opening of Houma's centennial celebration on Thursday, May 10, 1934. Despite drizzling rain, crowds gathered in Municipal Park to witness Mayor Elward Wright, Gov. O.K. Allen, and others start the four-day festivities. (Courtesy of the Cobb collection.)

9

The big parade of 1934 was held on Sunday, May 13, with the lead float honoring the first residents of Terrebonne Parish. Houma was named for the small band of Native Americans that called this area home. Their village was located at Ouiski Point, at the intersection of Bayous Cane and Black, about three miles northwest of downtown Houma. Their tribal name means "red" and is one of a few words of their language to survive. (Courtesy of TPCG.)

The village of Bourg was represented in the parade by their public school band. Like many unincorporated villages in the area, the school and its various activities instilled pride in the residents. Including the Bourg band insured a big turnout from this area located about 12 miles southeast of downtown Houma. (Courtesy of TPCG.)

This large American flag was hand carried along the parade route by representatives of every civic, public, and social organization in the area. It was handmade in 1917 by the ladies of the Houma Elks Lodge during World War I. It always stirred strong feelings of patriotism among the citizens. Spectators threw money into the flag as it passed in review, raising money to support our efforts for victory in 1918. (Courtesy of TPCG.)

The importance of Houma's seafood industry is depicted early in the centennial celebration parade. An oyster shell replica formed the backdrop for King Neptune's throne. He is surrounded by mermaids and maidens of the deep. (Courtesy of TPCG.)

Agriculture plays its part in Houma's history. The rich alluvial soil brought in by the annual Mississippi River spring floods combined with the temperate climate produces a large variety of products. These were shown as flowing from the cornucopia at the rear of the display. Young farm ladies dressed appropriately completed the tableau. (Courtesy TPCG.)

This float's theme is the value of education. Giant books form the backdrop for the graduates on the top tier. Younger children represent the lower grades. Each was identified by a particular subject that was part of the education program. School children from throughout Terrebonne Parish participated in the celebration. The "graduates" are Carl Nader and Bessie Blum. (Courtesy of TPCG.)

Although the nation was enjoying a period of peace, Houma had a smart looking and efficient National Guard unit. The young men of the unit trained regularly, on weekends, and were ready for any emergency, including the catastrophic flood of 1927. (Courtesy TPCG.)

Terrebonne Parish had many schools located in the unincorporated villages. Many had music programs that supported school bands. The village of Montegut was well represented by their smartly dressed school band. (Courtesy TPCG)

Oil was a welcome addition to the Houma economy. Until then, agriculture, seafood, and fur trapping drove the economy. Around the turn of the 20th century, Spindletop from Texas brought speculation of oil producing sands in Louisiana. This was established when production began in Jennings, Louisiana. By 1906, test borings showed slight traces of oil in Terrebonne Parish. Oil produced in this region in 1933 was 2,935,905 barrels. (Courtesy of TPCG.)

Terrebonne High School band in full array performs as part of the centennial celebration parade. Director Brooks Higdnis is in the foreground playing the coronet, wearing a coat and tie. The girls have capes and the boys have on shirts and ties. At that time, Terrebonne High School was the largest public school in the system and was located in downtown Houma. (Courtesy of TPCG.)

The Fabregas Junior Band was not affiliated with any school. Founded by Prof. Frank Fabregas in 1888, he sold the instruments and provided instructions on how to play them. As the students progressed, they joined the senior band. A tradition in Houma for many years, the Sunday afternoon Fabregas Band concerts were given in the band pavilion located under the oaks in the Main Street courthouse square. (Courtesy TPCG.)

The "cooperation" float brought the centennial celebration parade to a close. Although it was confined to farming, its meaning applied to the entire economy of Houma. A rainbow connects the production to the marketing. The skills are shown by the attire of the workers. Plows representing production are held by workers in overalls. Those in shirt sleeves represent the packers, or "middle men." The marketing is featured by men in suits and ties. The end product is represented by material packed in sacks. The whole process was dependent on each part, making each aspect as important as the others. Cooperation is the key to a bright future, as represented by the rainbow that united all the elements creating a major factor in the city's progress. (Courtesy of the Cobb collection.)

Texas Oil Company, which later became Texaco, had a commanding presence in the rising economy of Houma. As part of the centennial celebration, the latest additions to the growing organization were the tugboats to service Texaco's offshore oil operations. In this photo, the *Houma* is about to be christened prior to being put in service. Mayor T. Elward Wright is the man in white, wearing a hat. Others in the photo are Texaco and government officials. To add even more importance to the event, a large crowd gathered at dockside. (Courtesy of TPCG.)

The queen of the pageant "Leaves of Memory" is flanked by her court. The event, highlighting the history of Houma, was presented on Saturday evening, May 12, 1934, at the American Legion stadium and was followed by street dancing. Fifteen girls were chosen from the public and private schools in the city, including Alma Chauvin, who became queen when her name was drawn. In addition to Miss Chauvin, the group included Ernestine Boudreaux, Margaret Braud, Jeanette Ellender, Helena Foolkes, Ora Alice Gouner, Nita Jackson, Bettie LeBlanc, Marie Ledet, Ruth Pellegrin, Carol Lee Tucker, Brunella Voisin, Juanita Walton, Nan Watkins, and Felicie Wurzlow. Over 600 school children and their teachers were involved in the production. (Courtesy of Alma Chauvin Richard.)

Sunday, May 13, 1934, was the final day of the event and featured a barbecue and picnic on the grounds of the American Legion Park, followed by the parade. The day was designated as "homecoming day" and an invitation was given to former residents to be a part of the celebration. Note the pit, which was supported by iron legs resting on a wire rack. (Courtesy of TPCG.)

Here is Lafayette Street at its intersection with Main Street in downtown Houma. The city had recently benefited from funds made available by the Works Progress Administration (WPA). This was part of President Franklin Roosevelt's "alphabet soup" program to relieve the nation of effects of the depression. Houma used the money to improve streets in the downtown area from shell to concrete, helping to make the centennial celebration a success. (Courtesy of TPCG.)

Students, teachers, and employees of the Montegut School assembled in Shady Oaks Park in downtown Houma in May 1934 in preparation for the centennial celebration. The group included the school band with instruments as they prepared to march in the parade. All schools in the parish participated. (Courtesy of TPCG.)

Boy Scout Troop 306 played a large part in the centennial celebration. Here, they are shown assembled on the steps of city hall. Those identified are H.P. St. Martin Jr. (front row, holding his hat), Joseph Blum (far right, holding hat), and Allen Ellender Jr., who is directly behind Blum. Percival Davidson Jr. stands in uniform on the front row, third from left. (Courtesy of TPCG.)

Houma's new city hall was dedicated as part of the centennial celebration. The building was originally the People's Bank and was acquired and renovated by the city. Houma's police department and city marshal occupied the rear of the building. The mayor, city clerk, and council chambers were located in the front Main Street entrance. (Courtesy of TPCG.)

Thomas Elward Wright, first elected mayor in 1928, is credited with conceiving the idea of a centennial celebration. He started its organization and pushed it to a successful conclusion. He had just been reelected to a new four-year term. He remained mayor through 1946, when a new slate of officials replaced his administration. (Courtesy of TPCG.)

Two of the participants in the centennial hold the official flag of the event. This 1968 photo shows Leopold Blum on the left, who served as city alderman of the third ward (downtown Houma) from 1928 through 1946. He rode on the Seafood Float as King Neptune. On the right, Leon Bauland chaired the decorating committee. He was responsible for storefront banners, flags, and bunting along the parade route. (Courtesy of the Cobb collection.)

Two

LEADERS
AND LANDMARKS

The 1896 town council of Houma posed for their official photograph. Note the painted forest backdrop. From left to right are the following: (front row) Ald. Edwin Clarence Wurzlow, Mayor Joseph Cyrille Dupont, and Ald. Louis Lewald; (back row) Town Marshall J. Posey Campbell, Ald. William Wright Jr., Ald. Rudolph Louis Zelenka D.D.S., City Clerk Dreaux Angers, Ald. Emile Daigle Jr., and Assistant Marshall F.X. Zeringer. According to the census of 1900, Houma had a population of 3,212. This photo was taken in May 1897, shortly after Dreaux Angers assumed the position of city clerk. He remained there for over 40 years, until his health forced his retirement. (Courtesy of the Cobb collection.)

The town council of Houma posed for this photo in 1908 on the entrance steps to the Terrebonne Parish Courthouse. From left to right are the following: (front row) City Marshall F.X. Zeringer, Mayor Calvin Wurzlow, Ald. Clifford P. Smith, and City Clerk Drew Angers; (back row) Ald. Winslow G. Hatch; Assistant Marshall Felix A. Webre, Assistant Marshall Louis A. Chauvin, Treasurer Alphonse Dupont, Ald. Hugo Kahn, Ald. A.J. Bethancourt, and Ald. Harry Hellier. By the census of 1910, Houma had a population of 5,024. (Courtesy of the Cobb collection.)

Posed for their official photo in 1940, members of the city council, from left to right, are (front row) Alderman-at-Large Louis C. LeBlanc, Mayor T. Elward Wright, Ald. Allen Munson, and Ald. Harry Hellier; (back row) City Clerk William Drott, Chief of Police C.A. Callahan, Ald. Leopold Blum, and Ald. William Cenac. The population at this time was approximately 10,000. (Courtesy of the Cobb collection.)

26

With its four-face clock, the
Terrebonne Parish courthouse in
downtown Houma was a landmark
from the time the original building
was constructed in 1860. It was
remodeled in 1892. The parish jail was
in a separate building right behind
the main structure. The gallows
for carrying out death sentences
by hanging were located on the
third floor. This building was torn
down in 1937 to make way for the
present courthouse. (Courtesy of the
Cobb collection.)

The Terrebonne Parish police jury (the governing body) is shown in their courthouse meeting room on May 10, 1932. The parish was defined by mostly unincorporated villages. Each juror was responsible for the area in his ward. Standing from left to right are jurors Willis Pellegrin, Elgin J. Blanchard, Dr. Marcelin V. Marmande, J.G. Duplantis, Claude P. Boudreaux, and Alidore Mahler. Seated from left to right are Secretary-Treasurer O.J. Theriot, Pres. William McCollam, and jurors Charles L. Chauvin, D.C. McIntire, and Sam Polmer. (Courtesy of the Cobb collection.)

Here is Houma's town hall and fire station showing the new 1918 model American LaFrance fire engine. Albert Doiron is at the wheel. Originally built in 1857 to house a public market, the structure was used to house the fire equipment, chief of police office, and city court. Note the brick piers extending from ground level to the second floor. When demolished in 1930, an iron box containing two silver coins, a half dime, and a dime, dated 1854, were found along with an old newspaper and a wine bottle whose cork had deteriorated. The building was located on the property donated to the city when Houma was founded in 1834. It stood on the Bayou Terrebonne side of Main Street across from Courthouse Square. (Courtesy of TPCG.)

Houma's first municipal-owned electric generator was installed in a Main Street facility especially built in 1909 to house this modern marvel. Situated on the bank of Bayou Terrebonne, it allowed water to be electrically pumped for fire protection. The generator was installed and maintained by the Southern Electrical Manufacturing and Supply Co. Ltd., located in New Orleans. (Courtesy of the Cobb collection.)

Houma's incinerator was constructed with funds obtained from the Federal Government's Public Works Administration in 1935 on public property at the corner of Honduras and Roussell Streets. It was demolished to make way for the present city jail and police department. The trash wagon has just dumped its load into the fire chamber. (Courtesy of TPCG.)

As the population increased, so did the need for city provided utilities. The new electric generating facility was located on Barrow Street at what was then the end of town. It replaced the Main Street facility in 1928. The new facility housed three new generators. (Courtesy of TPCG.)

Additional generators were installed in 1950 and the facility was enlarged to accommodate the rapid growth of the city following World War II. Shown here is the service road leading into the plant from Barrow Street. Part of the distribution system is in the foreground. (Courtesy of TPCG.)

The bandstand was an important part of Houma's Courthouse Square, a center of entertainment, especially for Sunday afternoon concerts. As other entertainment became available, the bandstand fell into disuse. Here it is in its final location after removal to the Legion Park grounds. The wooden baseball stadium is in the background. (Courtesy of TPCG.)

Construction on Houma's new Main Street post office began in 1935, as part of the Works Progress Administration construction program for public buildings. It was located on parish property that formerly housed the opera house, public market, and town hall. It was replaced by a new post office and federal building in the early 1980s. (Courtesy of TPCG.)

By 1934, Houma's fire department was housed in its new facility, built on what had been the site of the city barn and livestock facility. Horses, mules, and any stray animals picked up by city police were kept here until claimed by their owners. The brick tower in the foreground was built in 1902 to support a water storage tank used for fire protection in the downtown area. (Courtesy of TPCG.)

With construction starting in 1954, the new Houma Auditorium opened its doors in 1956. The city's Mardi Gras celebration with a royal court tableau was a factor in creating the new facility. In addition to the stage area, it had meeting rooms and a complete kitchen. The facility was used year round until the parish government built a new civic center at the beginning of the 21st century. (Courtesy of TPCG.)

The construction of Houma's new water treatment facility in the southeast part of town made this water tower necessary to serve the city's north side. Located on the grounds of Legion Park, it has served as a prominent landmark since its completion in 1935. (Courtesy of TPCG.)

The picture shows Houma's tree-shaded Main Street looking west. The large brick building on the right housed the bus station at the corner of U.S. Highway 90 (Barrow Street). This served as the main highway entrance to the town. Newcomers were greeted with this scene during the 1930s. A car is entering Spahr's Texaco Station. (Courtesy of TPCG.)

Here is Houma's busy Church Street, looking south from its intersection with Main Street. The tall spire of St. Francis de Sales Catholic Church gives the street its name. To the left is the courthouse with its front entrance on Main Street. Terrebonne High School is behind the church, facing Church Street. (Courtesy of TPCG.)

This is a newly paved Main Street looking east at the intersection with Barataria Street in 1934. The Elster family owned and operated a clothing store until the early 1980s. Directly across the street was Joseph Crispino's fruit stand, grocery, and bar. Like many early merchants, the family occupied the second-story living quarters. (Courtesy of TPCG.)

Sidney Spahr's Texaco Station was located on Main Street near its intersection with U.S. Highway 90. By the mid-1930s, Texaco was the leading oil producer in Terrebonne Parish. Their large work force assured the success of this business. The landmark later housed Lee Marcel's Yellow Cab Stand. (Courtesy of TPCG.)

The new Houma Airport was dedicated in May 1939. Located on property acquired from the Barrow Family, this was desirable due to the remote, uninhabited area, which was formerly a sugar cane field. Bayou Terrebonne is on the left as the highway follows it south toward the Gulf of Mexico. The landing area was accessed by a clamshell strip—there were no runways. (Courtesy TPCG.)

Mayor T. Elward Wright speaks from the back of a Texaco Truck to officially dedicate the airport. As the Texas Oil Company (Texaco) became more active in oil production, it required more support services. The new air service helped fill this need. By May of 1938, air mail service began linking the Houma area with the international community. (Courtesy of TPCG.)

Ground breaking for the new parish courthouse took place in May 1937 and was completed mostly with funds from the Federal Public Works Administration. Dedication festivities were held on Sunday, August 28, 1938. Turning the symbolic shovel is architect Joseph Bernard of the firm Wogan and Bernard. Others in the photo, from left to right, are police juror and building committee chairman Charles L. Chauvin, Police Jury Secretary/Treasurer O.J. Theriot, Mayor Elward Wright, Joseph Bernard, Police Jury Pres. Dr. Marcelin V. Marmande, and PWC Engineer Capt. Mason. (Courtesy of TPCG.)

Parish police jury members sat for their portrait in the third floor of the courthouse meeting room on April 10, 1957. Seated from left to right are Conrad Picou, Wallace Ellender, James Buquet Sr., Jury Pres. Thaddeus Pellegrin, Alvin Boudreaux, Royal Pellegrin, Easton Duplantis, and Nolan Rogers. Standing from left to right are Madison L. Funderburk, Elward T. Brady Sr., Eustice Guillot, Vital Porche, Charles Duet, Rivers Breaux, A.P. "Tenner" Cenac, Carol Breaux (assistant secretary), and Ralph Bisland (secretary treasurer.) (Courtesy of TPCG.)

A large crowd gathered at the corner of Academy and Grinage Streets in May 1931. It was the dedication of Houma's newest school. Built in the art nouveau style of the period, the two-story structure became known as Houma Elementary. It featured the latest technology in school buildings and initially housed grades three through five. (Courtesy of TPCG.)

Houma Elementary students of Rosalie Kelly's fifth-grade class of 1948–1949 pose on the steps of the main entrance. From left to right are the following: (first row) Judy Chaisson, Theresa Clement, Felicie Cenac, Susan Chauvin, Betty ?, Evelyn ?, Phoebe Chauvin, Katherine ?, Libby Bourgeois, and Marsha Brewster; (second row) Betty Dolores Boudreaux, Patricia ?, Marcelene ?, Dolores Boudreaux, Barbara Cenac, Barbara ?, Betty Chaisson, Rose Marie Breaux, and Virgie LeBouef; (third row) Harrison ?, Thaddeus ?, Anderson ?, Dale Carlos, John Boudreaux, John Collins, Henry Boudreaux, Donald Carlos, J.B. Breaux, and Robert Brignac; (fourth row) Robert B. Butler III, Tommy Cobb, Aristele ?, Charles Breaux, Rosalie Kelly, teacher, Mary Jane ?, Shirley ?, Sherry Allen, and Charlotte Breaux. (Courtesy of the Cobb collection.)

John Peter Beck, the entrepreneur who organized and built Houma's natural gas distribution system, relaxes on his front porch. Originally from East Orange, New Jersey, he saw an opportunity to restore natural gas to Houma and was awarded a 25-year franchise by the city on April 20, 1938. (Courtesy of the Cobb collection.)

By December 1939, Beck's natural gas system was a reality. Ald. William Cenac's home on Park Avenue was the first installation. Attending the ceremony, from left to right, were (front row) Ald. Harry F. Hellier, Louis C. LeBlanc, David Olivier, Mayor T. Elward Wright, William Cenac, and Leopold Blum; (back row) City Clerk William Drott, unidentified, City Engineer T. Baker Smith, unidentified, and City Attorney J. Louis Watkins. (Courtesy of the Cobb collection.)

Houma was further linked to its neighbors by water with the completion of the Intracoastal Canal. By 1933, when the canal was dug through Main Street and Park Avenue, the city had not expanded much beyond the eastern side of the canal. A pontoon bridge connected East and West Houma. It soon became apparent as Houma expanded that a better facility was required. The dedication of the new drawbridge was held on May 16, 1937. (Courtesy of TPCG.)

The twin drawbridges connecting Main Street and Park Avenue were irritating to motorists as boat traffic on the Intracoastal was very heavy. A curfew was finally declared from 7 a.m. to 8 a.m. and from 5 p.m. to 6 p.m. on weekdays to allow motorists to pass and boats to wait. The local hospital was located on the west side and many east side babies were born in vehicles waiting for the bridge to close. (Courtesy of the Cobb collection.)

40

By 1937, Houma's residential area had expanded considerably on the north side of Bayou Terrebonne. A large event occurred in May with the completion and dedication of the Lafayette Street Bridge. Mayor T. Elward Wright was photographed just prior to its completion. (Courtesy of TPCG.)

The first automobile to break the ceremonial ribbon on the new Lafayette Street draw bridge was a 1937 Ford V8 convertible. Note the oyster shell street pavers linking both sides of the bridge. The newly constructed home of Dr. and Mrs. T.I. St. Martin faces Park Avenue in the background. (Courtesy of TPCG.)

On hand in May of 1937 to celebrate the opening of a new Lafayette Street draw bridge, from left to right, are city of Houma Ald. Leopold Blum, William Cenac, Harry Hellier, Louis LeBlanc, and Mayor T. Elward Wright. The bridge connected Lafayette Street to Park Avenue on the north side of Bayou Terrebonne. This proved to be a vital link in the expansion of the city northward. (Courtesy of TPCG.)

By 1968, Bayou Terrebonne had been declared non-navigable from New Orleans Boulevard in downtown Houma to its source in Thibodaux at Bayou Lafourche. Police juror Charles Duet suggested a couplet system to link the roads on both sides of the bayou. This photo shows construction of the fixed span in downtown Houma linking Roussell, Main, Park, and Suthon Streets. (Courtesy of TPCG.)

Houma has always been surrounded by waterways, but by the 1930s, it had outgrown its source of drinking water. Most residents used rainwater caught in large, round, wooden tanks called cisterns. Some still exist today. In 1936, the city built an electrical generating plant, a reservoir, and a water purification plant. Shown are members of the city government observing water being pumped from the Intracoastal Canal. (Courtesy of the Cobb collection.)

By 1968, piped purified water was available throughout Terrebonne Parish. It was accomplished with the building of an additional plant in the eastern part of the parish. A series of water towers maintained equal pressure. The Little Caillou Fire Company is shown putting water to good use. (Courtesy of TPCG.)

An overall view of downtown Houma in 1936 was taken shortly before the destruction of the old courthouse (foreground) and its four-faced clock. The jail is the separate building to the left and the Oak Tree Square is to the right. The triangle known as "Smoky Row" stands out from the square. The building with the tower on the bank of Bayou Terrebonne is the Knights of Pythias Lodge Hall. Main Street was paved, while Park Avenue on the north side of the bayou was not. Use of the waterways still played an important part in the city's economy, but as roads were paved and improved, the use of automobiles and trucks gained importance. Note the Paddlewheel Steamboat *N.H. Breaux* docked at the Daigle Barge Line wharf at the upper left. (Courtesy of TPCG.)

Three

GOOD EARTH PEOPLE

Houma's three wise men, from left to right, were Claude H. Wallis, Judge Robert B. Butler, and Rev. John N. Blackburn. A respected member of the community, Wallis was postmaster when the Republican Party was in control. With the election of Franklin Roosevelt to the presidency, Wallis joined the Houma recreation department as director of Shady Oaks Park. Butler was elected first to the Louisiana legislature and then to the District Judgeship in 1921. Blackburn ministered to the Presbyterian congregation. Upon Reverend Blackburn's retirement, the community honored him and his wife with a new home and automobile as a token of his service to all, regardless of their creed. (Courtesy of the Cobb collection.)

The Court House Square was the assembly area for this 1895 Houma Parade. Note the newly planted oak trees and picket fence. The Fabregas Band is in full dress. The riders are also in full regalia and are carrying flower bouquets. Even the bystanders are dressed for the occasion, hats included. A lone lad stands behind the fence, far removed from the scene. Behind him can be seen the wooden walkway leading to the main entrance of the courthouse. Parades have always been big in downtown Houma and are usually treated as family events. (Courtesy of TPCG.)

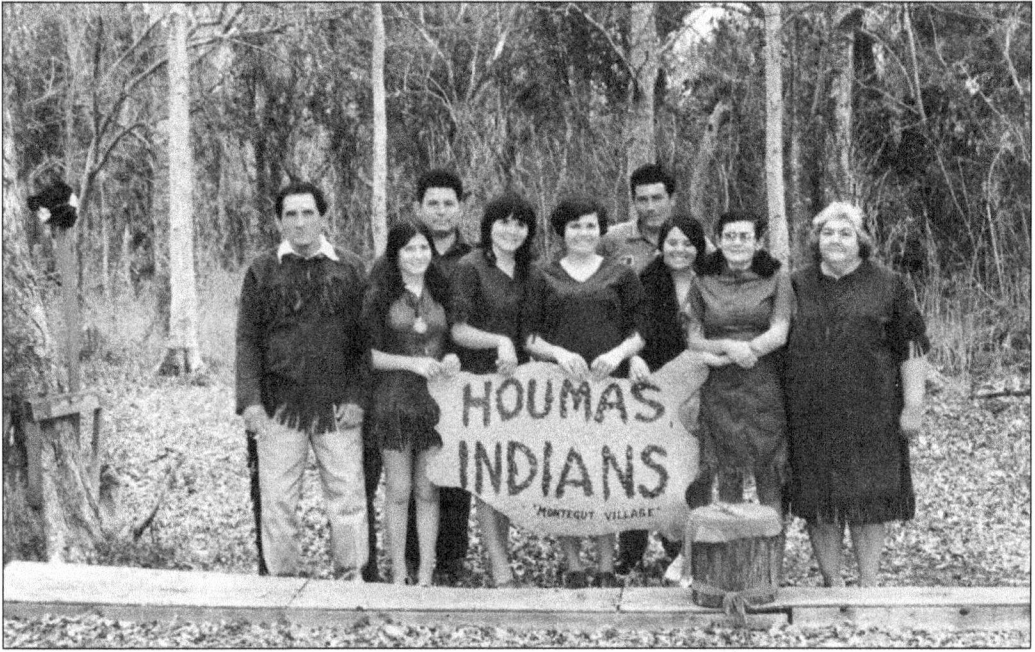

The Courteaux Family of Houmas Indians belongs to the Montegut Village of lower Terrebonne Parish. Jim, the chief, is the grandson of Rosalie Courteaux, one of the last great chiefs of the Terrebonne Indian village. The family shared their history, arts, and crafts in booths and demonstrations. They contributed everything they had been taught to preserve the traditions and lifestyle of their tribe. (Courtesy of the Cobb collection.)

To showcase the importance of truck farming in the Houma/Terrebonne area, an agriculture tour was held in l932. Sponsored by the chamber of commerce, a large group of elected officials, business leaders, and farmers toured the parish to showcase the readily available farm products. Most were shipped by rail and truck throughout the country. Included in this industry was a large canning plant, which processed much of the homegrown products. (Courtesy of TPCG.)

Due to the lack of ice, shrimp drying was essential to the preservation of the catch. The freshly caught catch was boiled in salt water and then spread on wooden platforms and allowed to dry in the sun. In the case of sudden or unforeseen rain, the catch was covered with canvas. Workers used wooden rakes, as shown, to stir the catch and insure uniform drying. (Courtesy of the Allen J. Ellender Archives, Ellender Memorial Library, Nicholls State University, Thibodaux, Louisiana.)

Party boats provided family outings, particularly on Sundays and holidays. Clifford Smith, his family, and friends, all in their Sunday best, are leaving the dock on Bayou Terrebonne at Barrow Street. Since the roads were not always passable, the boat provided a dependable means of transportation in the early 20th century. (Courtesy of Wm. Clifford Smith.)

This 1900 street fair was hosted by the merchants of downtown Houma. Various booths, flying horses housed under canvas, and a Ferris wheel drew large crowds. Since the fair was held on January 22, it is not surprising to see folks in coats and hats. The "Bull Durham" sign on the side of the Standard Drug Store building advertises a chewing tobacco popular at the time. (Courtesy of the Cobb collection.)

The Terrebonne High School graduating class of 1915 included, from left to right, (front row) Delphine Levy, Harris Berger, Gladys Porter, Samuel W. Pertuit, Thelma Zelenka, Everett Richardson, and Marguerite Wurzlow; (middle row) Olympe Darcey, Willard ?, Pearl Prejean, Abe Bergeron, Eudora Belanger, and Easton Duval; (back row) Lawrence Porche, Adele ?, Class Victorian Chloe Jones, Claude Guidry, Ovide Chauvin, Floyd Bourg, and Marie Bonvillian. Not pictured are Harry Vaughn and Beatrice Clement. (Courtesy of the Cobb collection.)

Terrebonne High School's first football team was organized in 1913. Proudly posed, from left to right, are (front row) Morris LeCompte, Dewey Daspit, Harris Berger, Roland Porche, and Allen LeCompte; (middle row) Abe Bergeron, Sam W. Pertuit, Floyd Bourg, Capt. Lawrence Porche, and Clay Dupont; (back row) Albert LeCompte, Alex Connelly, and Easton Duval. (Courtesy of the Cobb collection.)

Tristam B. Easton was a colorful character on the Houma scene. He purchased the *Houma Courier* from his cousin, Easton Duval, in 1909. He was the editor and publisher for the next 28 years. Having been a part of the town's political scene, he decided to sell the paper in 1937 and seek political office. He retired after an unsuccessful campaign for the state house of representatives in 1938. (Courtesy of the Cobb collection.)

Pictured here is John B. Gordon in 1961 at his desk as publisher of the *Houma Courier*. He arrived in January 1937 to become co-publisher and editor. A native of Oklahoma, he made Houma his home until his death 29 years later in 1976. During this time, he built the newspaper from a weekly circulation of 175 to a biweekly with a circulation of 12,000. Unfortunately, poor health forced his retirement and sale of the paper in 1970. (Courtesy of the Cobb collection.)

This happy group includes board members of the Houma Chapter of the National Conference of Christians and Jews. They were very active in Terrebonne from the 1950s through the 1970s, when local interest waned. Among their activities was the annual observance of "Brotherhood Week" and youth seminars, which they sponsored in the area high schools. Seated is board chairman W.J. "Bill" Davis. Those standing, from left to right, are Louis Miller, Sybil Martinez, Emanuel Geiger, Tracy Duplantis, Effie Breaux, Leo Ferber, and executive director Joseph Murphy. (Courtesy of the Cobb collection.)

The ladies of Houma enjoyed getting together for a game of cards and also looked forward to dressing up and going out for the afternoon with friends. This group, assembled during the Yule Season of 1956, from left to right, included Lillian C. McKnight, Eva B. Zelenka, Victoire M. Breaux, and her sister Marie M. Menville. (Courtesy of the Cobb collection.)

In 1954, Houma's business and community leaders hosted a meeting to hear Alton Ochsner, the world famous surgeon and founder of New Orleans-based Ochsner Foundation Clinic and Hospital. Dr. Ochsner had recently discovered a direct link between smoking and cancer. He established a series of meetings to inform the public of the dangers of smoking. Houma, with its close proximity to New Orleans, was one of his first presentations. Some of those attending, from left to right, were (seated) Main Street merchant Leo Ferber, Dr. Alton Ochsner, and his associate, Dr. Merril O. Hines; (standing) Assistant Superintendent of Terrebonne Schools C.C. Miller, insurance executive Jimmie Funderburk, School Superintendent Henry Louis Bourgeois, and Terrebonne police jury member Royal Pellegrin. (Courtesy of the Cobb collection.)

Bridges have always been important to downtown Houma, as Bayou Terrebonne flows straight through the heart of the city. In 1899, Houma moved across the bayou to the north bank. By 1906, the primitive wooden pedestrian bridge on Church Street gave way to the first iron span. It had been a railroad bridge and was brought in from another location. Standing on the newly completed bascule-type bridge, which was completed in 1940, from left to right, are Bill Dickerson (the superintendent for the Austin Bridge Co.), engineer S. Allen Munson, and engineer T. Baker Smith. (Courtesy of Wm. Clifford Smith.)

During the 1949 Christmas season, the Terrebonne Literary Club sponsored a Christmas play, which was held during their meeting at the Shady Oaks Park Center. Seated in the front row, with their backs to the camera, are Mrs. Myrtle K. Maier, her daughter Edith, Leopold B. Babin, and mother Sarah Babin. Standing, from left to right, are (front row) Ann Collins and William Pardington; (middle row) Martha Collins, Logan Babin Jr., Van Ellender, Nita Grace Pettigrew, Ann Rhea, Katherine O'Neal, and H. Sanders O'Neal; (back row) Alan Maier, McCauley Johnson, Wm. Clifford Smith, Ruth Abbot, Ernestine Ellender, Ann Barker, Jeannie Barker, and Tommy Cobb. (Courtesy of the Cobb collection.)

In July of 1954 the Citizens National Bank held an open house in its new building on Main Street. Representatives of the local government, bank board members, officers, and wives, posed for this picture. They represented some of the city's most important business leaders of the time. Seated, from left to right, are Mrs. Hugh St. Martin, Mrs. Butley Mahler, Mrs. Sam Scurto, Mrs. Madison Funderburk, and Mrs. Joseph Munson. Pictured standing, from left to right, are (front row) Mayor and Mrs. Leon Gary, Mrs. Louis Routier, Leopold Blum, Mrs. William Price, bank Pres. Madison Funderburk, Mrs. Ruby Thibodaux, Sam Scurto, D.C. McIntire, Harry Bourg, and William Price; (back row) Louis Routier, Dr. Hugh P. St. Martin, Ruby Thibodaux, Joseph J. Munson, and Parish Policy Jury Pres. Butley Mahler. (Courtesy of the Cobb collection.)

The 1912 graduating class of the Lorton Preparatory School assembled at the school entrance for their class portrait. Pictured from left to right are the following: (front row) Amalia Lewald (valedictorian) and Cecile Menville; (middle row) Helen S. Smith, Sarah Winder (teacher), and Viola Theriot; (back row) Jasper K. Wright, Virginia Pullen, Ester Wilson, Irene Aitkens, Sadie Celestin, and William McCollam. (Courtesy of the Cobb collection.)

Lorton Preparatory School students posed for this 1915 group portrait. Lorton was a private school founded and was staffed by the Winder sisters, Louise, Nina, and Sarah. Seated from left to right are May Sanders, J.C. Dupont Jr., Herbert Gray, Ruth Wright, Fanny Bonvillain, and Elsie Bonvillain. Pictured standing, from left to right, are Judith Theriot, Isare Cenac, Dewey Watkins, Albert Aucoin, Lavinia Connelly, Mildred Smith, Hanson Dupont, Lottie Sanders, Marie Duhon, and Francis Pullen. (Courtesy of Alice Steinkamp.)

Football and teenage boys went together like sunny days and recess in Houma. This was the 1912 "Bull Dog Flour" team on their playing field. From left to right are the following: (front row) Albert Cantrelle, Sidney Spahr, Tony Grasso, Bob Dupont with football, unidentified, Tom Dupont, and Carol Dupont; (back row) Jim Berger, Ralph Bisland, Rudolph Zelenka Jr., and J.C. Dupont Jr. (Courtesy of the Cobb collection.)

Sand lot baseball was popular during the 1930s. Notice the team mascot. None of the players are identified; however, some wear "Houma" shirts. It was not until 1946 that the Houma Indians team was organized and professional baseball came to town. The team was a member of the Evangeline League and played home games in the large wooden stadium located in the American Legion Park, now the site of Legion Park School. (Courtesy of the Cobb collection.)

J.W. Bojarsky was an immigrant merchant from Russia. He made his mark on Houma's Main Street, managing the "Houma Bargain Store" for over 40 years. Founded in 1910 by Leon Heyman, Bojarsky became manager when Heyman moved to New Orleans. His warm personality so endeared him to his customers that eventually the store was referred to as "Bojarsky's." When it closed in 1970, the property was given to the city of Houma. (Courtesy of Carolyn Lewald.)

Willie Hamilton was Terrebonne's blacksmith. We see him here in his Sunday suit ready to attend Catholic Mass. Originally from a sugar plantation in Convent, Louisiana, located on the Mississippi River, he settled in lower Terrebonne Parish at Sara Plantation in 1900. In 1908, he purchased property in east Houma and became a fixture in his shop on Main Street. Assisted by two of his sons, Allen and Peter, the Hamiltons saw to the needs of the sugar, seafood, and oil industries in the area. (Courtesy of Allen Hamilton.)

Here is Thelma Zelenka as she appeared in 1922. A graduate of Terrebonne High School, she went to college at Louisiana Normal, later Northwestern State College in Natchitoches, Louisiana. After receiving her degree, she returned to become principal of the Bourg Public School. She later returned to Northwestern State College as a professor of health and home economics. She met and married John S. Kyser, who eventually became Northwestern's president. (Courtesy of the Cobb collection.)

Dr. Rudolph Zelenka Jr., a popular Houma dentist, stops the vegetable wagon. This was a common sight on Houma's streets. The vendors obtained merchandise from area farmers, or from the French Market in New Orleans, and peddled from street to street. At first, they shouted their wares. Later, they rang large bells. With the advent of the motor truck, a horn sounded their arrival. The "super markets," with their large, refrigerated selection, sounded the death knell for this method of obtaining fresh vegetables. (Courtesy of the Cobb collection.)

Alphonse Authement takes a break on the steps of his Grand Caillou general merchandise store and lunch room. The store bearing his name was the center of life in this small fisherman's community. Here, supplies were provided in exchange for the fresh shrimp caught in the lakes and bays bordering the Gulf of Mexico. The catch was then processed by drying, canning, and later, freezing. Once sold, more supplies were purchased and the process repeated itself. (Courtesy of the Cobb collection.)

Two grand dames of Houma view the new classroom in the St. Francis de Sales Parochial School in downtown Houma. The building opened in 1952, when this photo was taken. At left is Mrs. James Chauvin, nee Minnie Jolet, Mrs. Louis Menville, and nee Victoire Gouaux. Both were lifelong members and workers in the St. Francis Catholic congregation. Mrs. Menville was particularly proud of the two-piece suit she knitted herself. (Courtesy of the Cobb collection.)

Local photographer Lee Webb took this prize-winning portrait of Judge Robert B. Butler. It won high honors when entered in a contest sponsored by the Professional Photographers of America and became part of their permanent collection, traveling through the country. Many attorneys in his court room watched as Judge Butler lit up and, as time passed, wondered how short he could smoke his cigar without catching his beard on fire. Those witnessing the spectacle for the first time were easily distracted from the business at hand. (Courtesy of the Cobb collection.)

Police jury (parish government) Secretary and Treasurer Odressis J. Theriot was a fixture in the Terrebonne Parish Courthouse from 1917 to 1951. A descendant of early settlers, he was born and raised in the Bayou Dularge community bearing his family name. Originally, Theriot was a dealer in cypress lumber, both rough and dressed. He served two terms on the board of aldermen, from December 1898 to July 1900. He is shown here on the occasion of his retirement sitting in his backyard in downtown Houma, a block from the courthouse. (Courtesy of the Cobb collection.)

Huey Long and his Houma supporters were assembled in front of the Rhodes Hotel on Main Street in downtown Houma. The newly elected governor had scheduled a rally in the courthouse square for 10:00 a.m. on Sunday, August 4, 1929. It is likely that the group walked the one block distance to attend the political meeting to help elect the Democratic nominee for congress. The group includes city and parish business leaders as well as members of a baseball team on their way to their Sunday game. From left to right are the following: (front row) J.G. Duplantis Sr., Harry Hellier, Sam Achee, Allen J. Ellender Sr., Joseph Jaccuzzo, Julius Dupont, Mayor T. Elward

Wright, Calvin Wurzlow, Gov. Huey P. Long, School Board Pres. Albert Viguerie, Police Jury Pres. Sam Polmer, Camille C. Duplantis, Gibson J. Autin Sr., James Kohmann, Albert Dupont, Joseph Malbrough, Adrien Caillouet, and Robert D. Lottinger; (back row) Sheriff F.X. Bourg, Vic Polite, Reubin Elster, George Matranga, Milton Toppino, Floyd Bascle, Freddie Hoffman, Frank Williams Sr., Edward Cheramie, Tris Easton, Claude P. Boudreaux, "Stonewall" Fanguy, and William Fakier. (Courtesy of Mrs. Audrey Autin Buquet.)

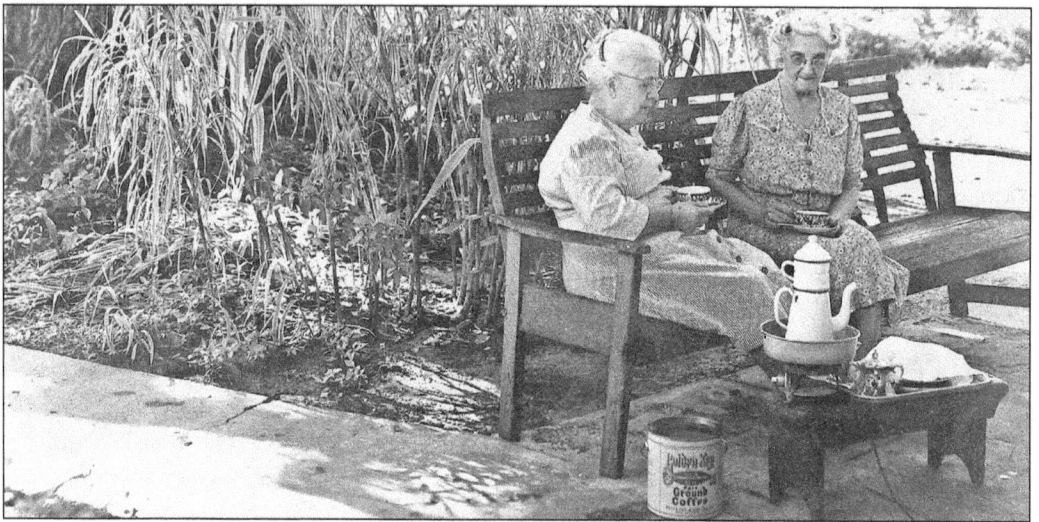

The happenings of the day were regularly exchanged over afternoon French-dripped coffee. Weather permitting, the neighbors sat outside with their coffee pot placed in hot water to keep warm. Seated here are Mrs. Odressis J. Theriot (left) and Mrs. Rudolph Zelenka (right). They are in the Theriot home's back yard, which adjoined the Zelenka homestead in downtown Houma. (Courtesy of the Cobb collection.)

Shown here are Terrebonne Parish welfare personnel and members of the Welfare Board in 1937. From left to right are (seated) Lorna Daspit (intake worker), Eva Bourg (field worker), Josie Oliver (field worker), Victorine Chauvin (field worker), and Jeanne G. Wurzlow (office secretary); (kneeling) Marie Elise Duplantis (stenographer), Bertha M. Lirette (stenographer), and Mrs. Verna G. Dean (field worker); (standing) Aubin Buquet (board member) Alidore Mahler (board chairman), Frances St. Martin (parish director), Mrs. Harold Dupont (board vice-chairman), Pearl Neal (field worker), Edwin Bourg (board member), Maria Acosta (field worker), and Wallace Ellender (board member). (Courtesy of the Cobb collection.)

Bob Verret stands in front of his store built on stilts, which was located on Lake Barre as part of a shrimp drying operation in lower Terrebonne about 1920. In addition to the store, which contained the necessities of life, the workers lived in cabins located on the platform. Verret provided the inspiration for Thad St. Martin's storekeeper in his novel *Madame Toussaint's Wedding Day*. (Courtesy of the Cobb collection.)

A typical general merchandise store of this era was located in Chacahoula at Bull Run Road. Standing behind the counter is storekeeper Edgar Guillot. The delivery lad is waiting for the box on the counter. The metal barrels contained kerosene for heating, cooking, and lighting. (Courtesy of Barbara Wurzlow Picard.)

Radio came to Houma in 1922 when Joe and Francis Pullen installed this receiver and transmitter in their downtown Houma home. They sought and received permission from the city council to use the nearby water tower to attach the aerial. The brothers later won a contract from the Lafourche Parish (Terrebonne's neighbor) School Board to teach radio to high school students. (Courtesy of the Cobb collection.)

By the 1950s, Joe Pullen's ham radio station W5ZAB was considerably more powerful—so much so that it interfered with the early Houma television reception, causing many complaints. In this photo, Pullen is allowing retired Judge Robert B. Butler Sr. to talk to Francis Pullen in Baton Rouge. The local Cub Scout den with their den mother (unidentified) pays close attention. (Courtesy of the Cobb collection.)

Mardi Gras celebrations have long been a tradition in Houma and Terrebonne Parish. The krewe captain is responsible for staging the tableau (pageant) ball and parade. In full costume for the 1965 Krewe of Terreanians event are George C. Fakier (captain) on the left and Elward T. Brady (king) on the right. His queen was Barbara Sinclair. (Courtesy of the Cobb collection.)

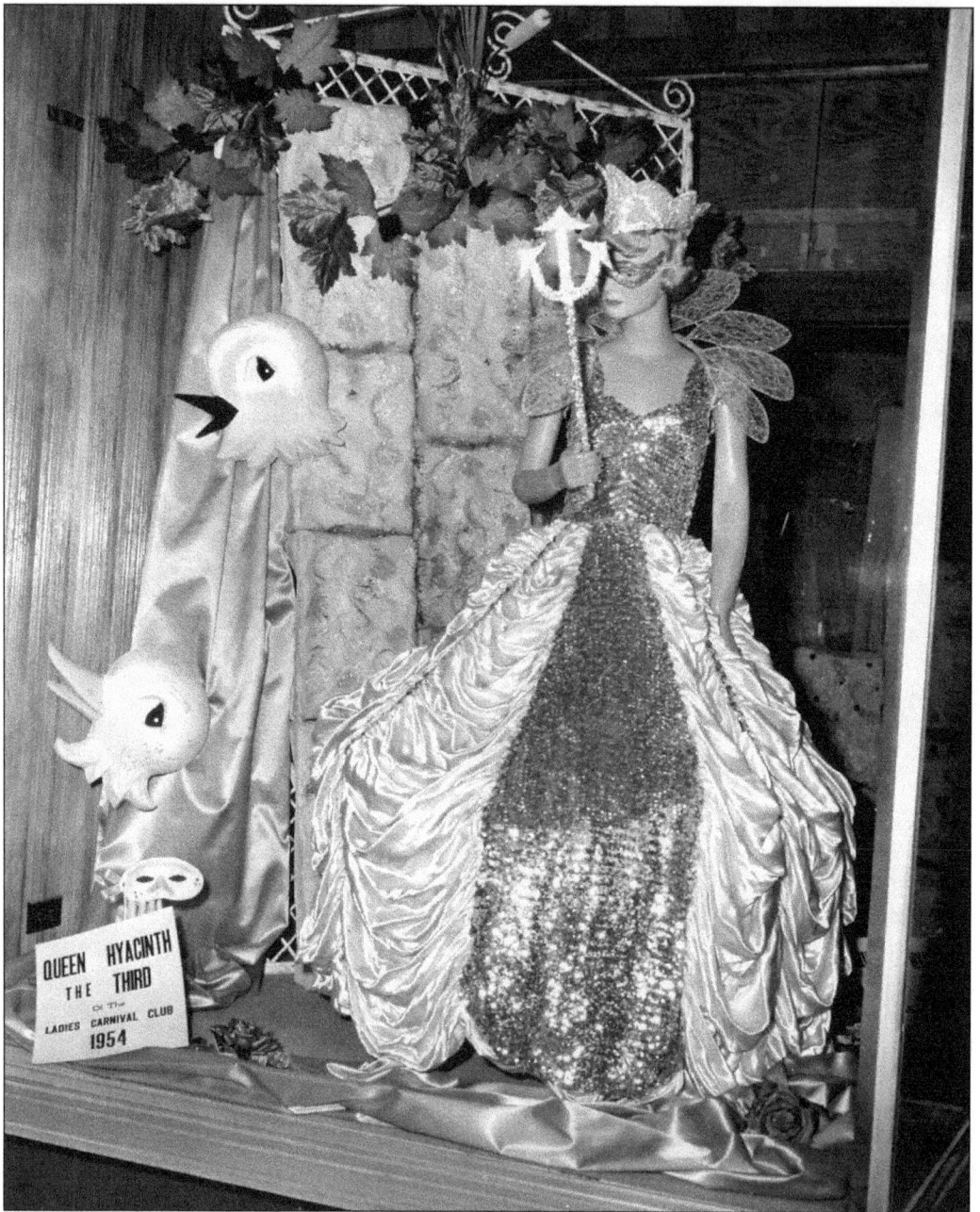

Costumes of past Houma Mardi Gras royalty were displayed in many Main Street store windows. This was the only way the public could view these beautiful creations up close. The "Ladies Carnival Club," one of the many krewes that parade annually, shows their 1954 queen's costume. These displays always created a lot of interest in the store windows. This costume belonged to Queen Alvita Acosta Randolph. (Courtesy of the Cobb collection.)

70

In January 1952, these Terrebonne beauties were the winners of the "Kedettes Casuals" shoe contest. The manufacturer sponsored the event through their local retailers to promote their line of shoes. Seated is Patsy Callahan holding an illustration of the Kedette Shoe Sole. Standing from left to right are Rosetta Fanguy, Joretta Achee, Geraldine Wallis, and Mary Claire Thibodaux. (Courtesy of the Cobb collection.)

These young ladies from the Houma area were the 1938 winners of the "Kedettes Casuals" shoe contest. From left to right are Mabel Hochendel, Wyonna Fortson, Marian Lirette, Lou Rhodes, and Dot King. It is interesting to note the dramatic difference in the shoe styles. (Courtesy of the Cobb collection.)

Weddings in the "Good Earth" are always a big celebration for family and friends. This is particularly true in the Bayou Country, where the homes have large yards. This outdoor wedding reception was held on Bayou Little Caillou in the 1930s. Note the long table leading to the front yard laden with food. (Courtesy of the Cobb collection.)

A bad day for the trout was a good day for these fishermen. Located within easy access of the fishing grounds off the coast of Louisiana, sportsmen have often returned to shore with a good catch. This group at their fishing camp included many Houma citizens. Pictured from left to right are the following: (front row) unidentified, Dr. Leon Menville, A.J. Bethancourt, and T. Baker Smith; (back row) Jasper K. Wright, two unidentified, and Dr. Hugh P. St. Martin. The rest are unidentified. (Courtesy of "Buckey" Starr.)

72

Big, Bad Betsy was the hurricane of 1965, with winds in downtown Houma exceeding 100 mph. The majestic court square oaks weathered the storm as they had since being planted in 1886. Life went on as usual for these Court Square bench sitters as cleanup crews surveyed what needed to be done to restore the area. The two sitters in the foreground are Mike Michel (left) and Levy Marcel (right), both court square regulars. (Courtesy of the Cobb collection.)

During hurricanes, residents of the low lying areas move to their boats in order to ride out the storms. In many areas, they are provided with very high moorings so that, as the waters rise and the storm surge comes, the boats will be safely secured. (Courtesy of the A.P. Cenac Family.)

Hurricane Carla devastated Terrebonne in September 1961. Roads in the lower areas were completely flooded, along with some vehicles. Small boats became the means of transportation. The Oaks Fishing Lodge remained open and continued to sell what supplies were on hand. The oak tree, suffering the repeated affects of salt water storm surges, merely serves as a mooring for boats. (Courtesy of the A.P. Cenac Family.)

Houma's "Order of Red Men" posed for this 1895 group assembly prior to their downtown parade. At that time, the Order of Red Men was one of the major benevolent and fraternal orders in America. They sought to emulate the high morals and ideals of the Native Americans. This photo shows them in full regalia, including their elaborate headdresses. Note the beautiful well-groomed horses and the large crowd of on-lookers in the rear. In addition to the Order of Red Men, Houma's men could join the Catholic Knights of America, Ancient O.V. Workmen, Knights of Honor, or the Knights of Pythias. (Courtesy of the Cobb collection.)

Houma's Home Guard is shown as they appeared in 1940. They posed at the Legion Park. It is identified by the water tower in the background. These men gave their time on weekends and were subject to being called out in times of hurricanes, large fires, or any other emergencies. They were a valuable addition to Fourth of July celebrations and other events and parades in the city. Many served wartime duty for their country. A close look at the front and second rows will reveal the identities of Larry delaBretonne, "Happy" Robichaux, Dr. Barry J. Barrodale, Thomas Holcombe, and George Fakier. (Courtesy of the Cobb collection.)

An early landmark in downtown Houma was the Wright Livery Stable and meeting hall. Located at the corner of Grinage and Belanger (formerly Court) Streets, this convenient area became the sought out spot to assemble for the latest news of the day. In the days before the automobile, Wright's maintained a lively livery business. (Courtesy of Meredith Wright.)

Terrebonne's 150th birthday was in 1972. A parish-wide celebration honored the event. Headquarters were in a recently closed Main Street clothing store. Dressed in period clothing posing at the headquarters, from left to right, are (front row) Randolph Bazet III, Thomas Cobb Jr., unidentified, Margaret Cobb, George Cobb, and Thomas Cobb Sr.; (middle row) Randolph Bazet Jr., R.A. Bazet Sr., Lloyd Amadee, unidentified, and Dick Raulinson; (back row) Bill McMichael, Roland Belanger, and unidentified. (Courtesy of the Cobb collection.)

Four

HOUMA HAPPENINGS

The 1880s marked the beginning of the end of "reconstruction" in Houma following carpetbag rulers of the Republican Party. The 1898 election returned the Democratic Party to local prominence. This Main Street parade celebrated by showing a rooster riding an elephant. The sign reads, "You can't buy the Creoles. We made a clean sweep." The parade made its way to the court square, where the elephant was burned in effigy. The wooden buildings escaped two big Main Street fires in 1887 and 1891, which destroyed the north side of the street. Rather than burn, they just smoked. The name "Smoky Row" is still used to describe this block. They were torn down in 1900 and replaced with fire-proof structures, as mandated in the new city ordinance. (Courtesy of Meredith Wright.)

On New Year's Day, 1949, a Main Street landmark was completely destroyed by fire. Caught by the photographer just as the blaze was discovered, the Rhodes Hotel was never rebuilt. The three-story Commercial Hotel next door remained unharmed. (Courtesy of Ivy Smith Sr.)

Saturday afternoon, January 24, 1970 will always be remembered by those who witnessed the explosion at the northwest corner of Main and Church Streets. Five buildings and three lives were lost in one of the worst events to happen in downtown Houma. A leaking gas line under the buildings at the north corner of Main and Church Streets was ignited by a spark from a jackhammer used by workers to locate the leak. Three city employees were killed in the resulting explosion and fire: Assistant Fire Chief Loren Bourg and city workers Howard Arcement and Peter Knight. It wasn't until January 30 that this part of downtown Houma was declared safe for the general public. (Courtesy of Ivy Smith Sr.)

President Richard Nixon is standing next to the bespectacled Sen. Allen J. Ellender of Louisiana during Ellender's 1972 campaign for reelection. Originally elected in 1936, Ellender began his public career shortly after graduating from Tulane School of Law. He was appointed city attorney for Houma on September 2, 1913. In 1924, he was elected to the Louisiana House of Representatives and became floor leader for Gov. Huey P. Long in 1928 and House Speaker in 1931. His election to the U.S. Senate to fill the position formerly held by Long was due to his popularity with the Huey Long political faction. (Courtesy of the Ellender Archives, Ellender Memorial Library, Nicholls State University, Thibodaux, Louisiana.)

In 1952 the Long legacy was very much a factor in Louisiana politics. Huey's brother Earl is shown on the day of his inauguration as governor for the third time. Frome left to right are U.S. senators Allen J. Ellender and Russel Long (Huey's son), Governor Earl Long, and Congressman George Long (Earl and Huey's brother). (Courtesy of the Ellender Archives, Ellender Memorial Library, Nicholls State University, Thibodaux, Louisiana.)

President and Mrs. Richard Nixon are shown being escorted into St. Francis de Sales Catholic Church in downtown Houma by Thomas Elward Wright for the funeral of Sen. Allen J. Ellender. Senator Ellender died suddenly on July 27, 1972, in the midst of his campaign for reelection. His funeral and burial were held on July 31. In addition to the Nixons, the service was attended by Vice President Spiro Agnew and his wife, Speaker of the House Carl Albert, and Senate Pres. Pro Tem James O. Eastland. Many state and national leaders were also in attendance. Houma was host to the greatest gathering of national officials in Louisiana history. (Courtesy of Cecele Edsburg.)

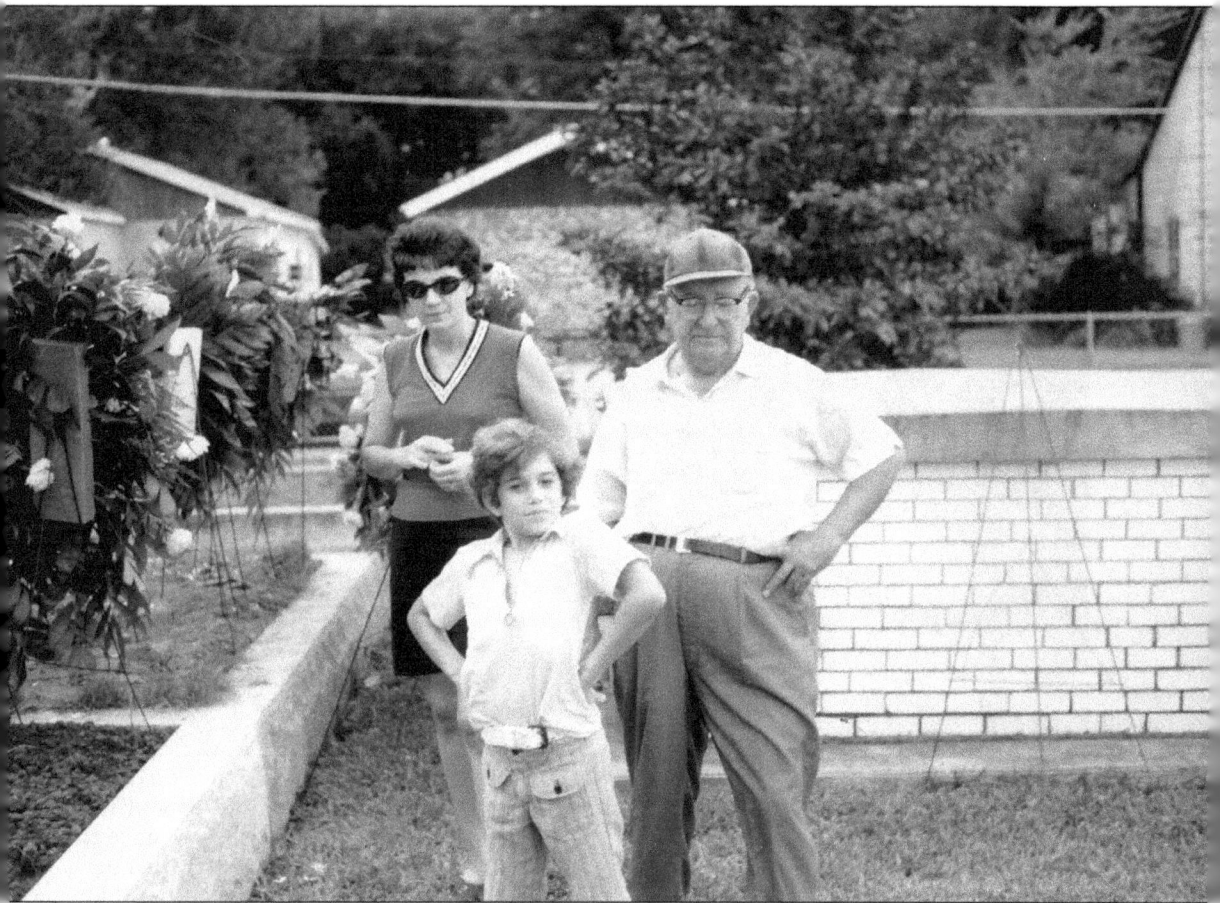

Visiting the gravesite of Sen. Allen J. Ellender, from left to right, are George F. Cobb (child), Janet E. Kyser, and Randolph A. Bazet. Ellender and Bazet became friends in 1916 when Ellender was practicing law and Bazet was assistant Terrebonne Parish clerk of court. They enjoyed each other's friendship to the extent that they purchased their burial sites side by side so they could share a common two-sided grave stone. Bazet went on to become clerk of court and was reelected until he chose to retire. (Courtesy of the Cobb collection.)

A heavy snowstorm closed Houma down on Wednesday, February 12, 1958. Not since the snow of February 1895 had such an event of nature occurred in the city. Schools, businesses, and government offices were closed, both out of necessity and to give residents an opportunity to enjoy the once-in-a-lifetime event. In addition to the snow, night-time freezing temperatures created ice in some parts of the parish's bayous. (Courtesy of the Cobb collection.)

The Cook-Hattaway home on Main Street in downtown Houma became the perfect setting of a winter wonderland following the snow storm of February 1958. Built entirely of virgin cypress in 1914 by lumber baron Herman Cook, the home contains a cellar in an area with a high water table. (Courtesy of the Cobb collection.)

The heavy snowfall in February 1958 completely transformed Houma's Courthouse Square. Due to freezing temperatures, snow remained for at least two days. The famed oak trees were unharmed. Their beauty was enhanced by the snow, which completely covered their foliage and the ground on which they still stand today. The courthouse was closed for a day so all employees could enjoy the transformation. Houma's Thatcher Hotel is in the background. (Courtesy of the Cobb collection.)

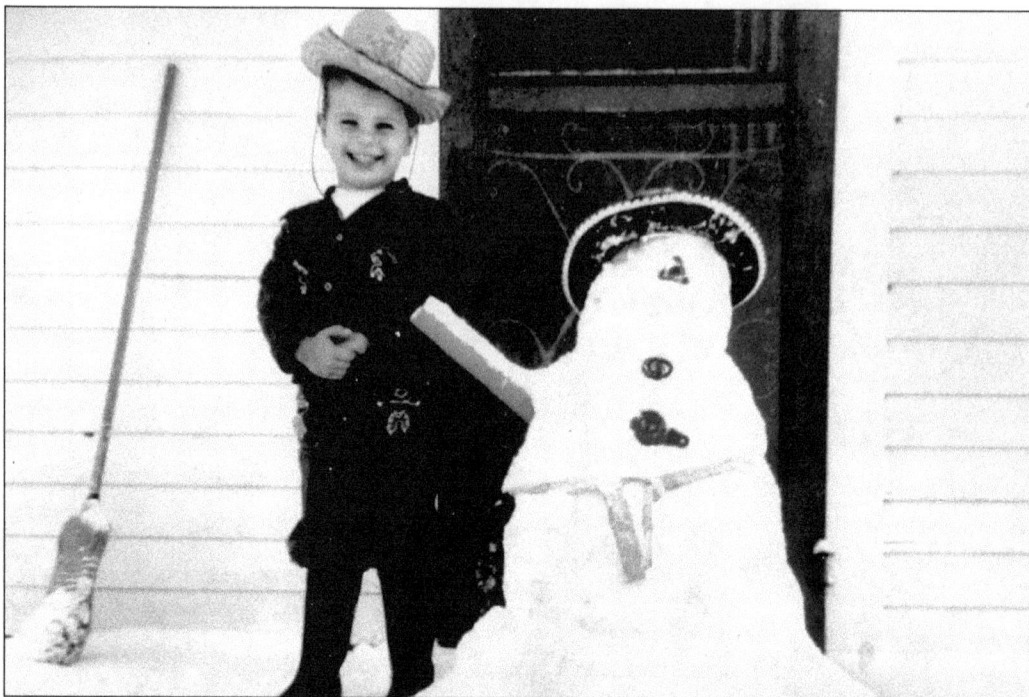

Children throughout Terrebonne had enough snow to build some good-sized snowmen. Kerry Legendre shows off his snow-covered front porch. Located in Gray, the small community in the northern part of the parish received a heavier accumulation. (Courtesy of Audrey Legendre.)

The Brooks-Thatcher home on School Street in downtown Houma wore its mantle of snow well. This beautiful cypress wood structure was built by Thomas Brooks in the 1870s. It was purchased by oil and gas businessman and hotel owner J. Hunter Thatcher in the 1920s and extensively renovated and modernized. (Courtesy of the Cobb collection.)

84

The Louis Menville home and its ancient oak tree were located in downtown Houma at 635 School Street. The recent snowfall covers the fern. The cypress raised structure is in typical Acadian architectural style with a center hall and top dormer window. The front porch and high ceilings give ample ventilation for South Louisiana's lifestyle. (Courtesy of the Cobb collection.)

The snow-covered Lionel Babin home on Main Street was built in the 1950s. It was constructed from material salvaged from the Belle Grove Plantation home, located on Bayou Black in Terrebonne Parish. Babin preserved many of the artifacts from this impressive antebellum mansion and incorporated them in his residence. (Courtesy of the Cobb collection.)

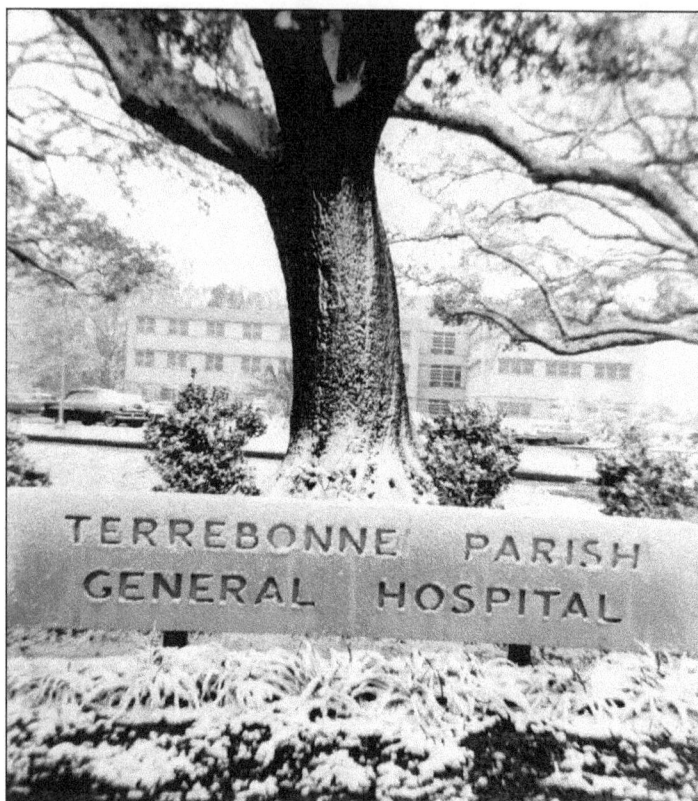

Terrebonne General Hospital, with its spacious grounds and historic oak, created a snow-covered winter wonderland, a phenomenon rarely seen in this tropical atmosphere. The hospital was constructed a mere four years before, in 1954, on Main Street property that had previously been the site of the Lucius F. Sutton home. (Courtesy of the Cobb collection.)

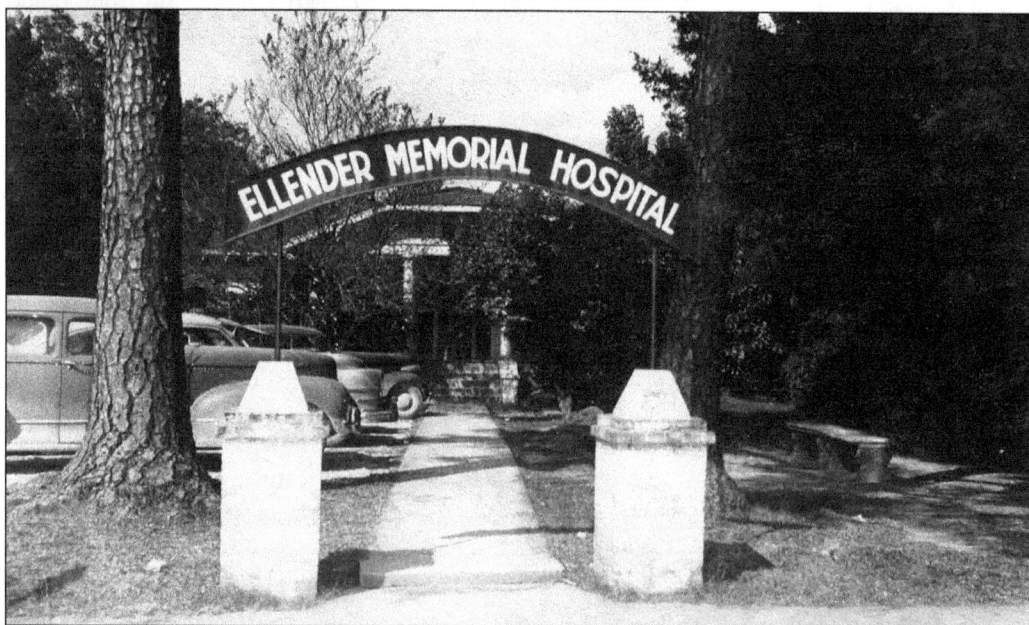

The predecessor to Terrebonne General was Ellender Memorial, opened in 1935 by physician cousins Willard and Ernest Ellender. The refurbished wooden building contained 22 beds. This was a private facility and provided medical attention to the area and served the needs of Terrebonne Parish for almost 20 years. (Courtesy of Ivy J. Smith.)

Leading the Mardi Gras parade of 1951 is King Houmas, A.R. Cenac Sr., as he waves to his royal subjects on downtown Houma's Main Street. The royal float is in front of the Bijou movie theater, one of four movie houses in the area. The parade floats had recently been pulled by horses and mules. This one uses a jeep. (Courtesy of the Cobb collection.)

Mardi Gras, or Fat Tuesday, gave residents the opportunity to be what they really wanted to be for one day only. This clown entertained parade goers on Main Street during the 1951 Mardi Gras festivities. He is standing in front of the "Houma Bargain Store" at the corner of Main and Roussell Streets. (Courtesy of the Cobb collection.)

A major event in the economic life of Houma and Terrebonne Parish occurred in May of 1936 with the completion of the Intracoastal Waterway through the area. The Houma-Terrebonne Chamber of Commerce marked the event with a reception and dedication ceremonies. The canal became invaluable during World War II when German submarines attacked the shipping lanes in the open waters of the Gulf of Mexico. The inland route extended from the East Coast to Texas. Shown on the front row, from left to right, are Farquard P. Guidry, banker; Harry Hellier, alderman; T. Elward Wright, mayor; George Harmount, Louisiana Agricultural Extension Service; and Madison L. Funderburk, banker. On the back row, from left to right, are Eugene Dumez, chamber of commerce manager; William J. Cenac, alderman; Emile Lapeyre, president of Grand Caillou Shrimp Packers; C.F. Richards of Kentucky, Inland Waterway Corp. board member; Col. Julius Dupont, chamber president; Col. John M. Hodges of St. Louis, Missouri, Inland Waterway Corp. board member; Albert M. Dupont, Houma merchant; General T.O. Ashburn, president of Inland Waterway Corp; Ozia Pellegrin, Houma businessman; and J.W. Mackie of Kansas, Inland Waterway Corp. board member. (Courtesy TPCG.)

Five

BUSINESS AND INDUSTRY

The *Higgins Hellcat* was considered the fastest P.T. boat to enter service during World War II. Although the Higgins's shipyard's main facility was located in nearby New Orleans on what is now Delgado Junior College, the shipbuilder established a location in Houma in early 1942. Using local labor, the plant produced landing craft and rocket launching landing craft support boats. With 175 employees, the production amounted to seven boats in six days. The finished boats were placed in the water and delivered to New Orleans under their own power. (Courtesy of Louis Blum Sr.)

In the early part of World War II, the department of the Navy established a blimp base on the outskirts of Houma, on property purchased from the R.R. Barrow family. This land was once a part of Roberta Grove sugar cane plantation. A large hanger and supporting facilities were built on earth that once provided sugar for the nation. The lighter-than-air blimps patrolled the Gulf of Mexico and provided protection from the German war machine. As a result of our war efforts, Houma had two German prisoner-of-war camps. The prisoners were used as field laborers by local farmers. At the conclusion of hostilities, the hangar was demolished and the base was utilized by NORAD, a part of the early warning defense system. In June 1957, the base was decommissioned and the property given to the Terrebonne Parish government for the peacetime use of the citizens. (Courtesy of C.J. Christ.)

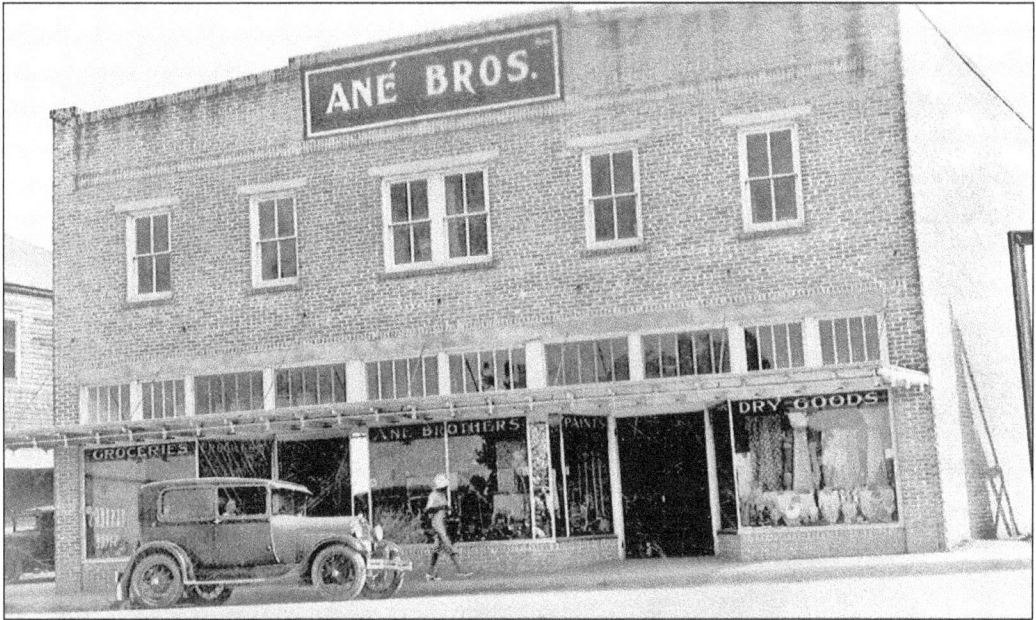

The Ane brothers, Joseph and Xavier, constructed their new facility in 1928 on Houma's Main Street. Located on what had been the Barataria Canal near its intersection with Bayou Terrebonne, it proved to be a valuable investment for the Houma businessmen who bought the canal right-of-way and filled it in. Others quickly bought lots on the filled-in canal facing the new streets, Barataria and Canal. (Courtesy of TPCG.)

The Seabreeze Restaurant was a Houma landmark at the corner of Main and Barrow Streets. Owned and operated by Junius Authement, the Seabreeze Hotel was located nearby, as was the Greyhound Bus Station. These facilities were usually the first encounter visitors arriving by bus had with Houma. The restaurant location also made it popular with Main Street business people and shoppers. (Courtesy of the Allen J. Ellender Archives, Ellender Memorial Library, Nicholls State University, Thibodaux, Louisiana.)

By the turn of the century, movies had come to Houma. The first, called Flickers, because the primitive equipment projected an uneven image, was located on the second floor of Houma's opera house on Main Street across from the court square. The Fox was built in 1936 and the Bijou in 1940. Both were located on Main Street in downtown Houma and were family owned, the Fox by William Cobb, James Chauvin, and Wallace Hepler, and the Bijou by Joseph Jaccuzzo, A.J. Bethancourt, and Henry Breaux. (Courtesy of the Cobb collection.)

The Houma Ice House was the first to manufacture ice and generate electricity for Houma residents. Built by Dr. Leon Jastremski in the 1890s, it served the community through the 1960s. The location on Bayou Terrebonne at the intersection of Church Street and Park Avenue enabled residents to obtain ice by land or by water. Independent routes were operated to supply home delivery. (Courtesy of TPCG.)

Houma's second ice manufacturer, Terrebonne Ice and Cold Storage, was established in the 1920s. It was a stock company composed of local investors. In addition to supplying ice to the area, residents could rent storage facilities to refrigerate their perishables. Packers could take advantage of market conditions to sell their inventories. The plant faced Park Avenue near the intersection of Suthon Avenue. (Courtesy of TPCG.)

Originally built in the 1920s as an apartment house, this building's owner, J. Hunter Thatcher, realized the need for a hotel in downtown Houma. Located on Goode and Belanger Streets, the main entrance faces the courthouse square. A&P, Houma's first supermarket, was located in part of the ground floor. In addition, the hotel boasted a restaurant and telegraph office. The four-story structure also featured an elegant lobby and elevator. (Courtesy of TPCG.)

Prof. Frank Fabregas opened his music store in downtown Houma in 1898. His son, Louis, and later his daughter, Rosa, operated the business. Here, she looks on while "Nipper" listens to his master's voice on the early model phonograph. The early recordings were round and made of wax. Along the wall is the store display of vinyl long-playing recordings. (Courtesy of the Cobb collection.)

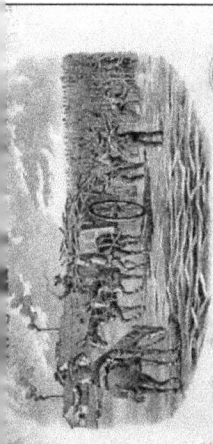

THE ARGYLE PLANTING & MANUFACTURING CO. LTD.

SUGAR MANUFACTURERS.

No. 1354

Houma, La. _____ 189__

PAY TO THE ORDER OF _____ $_____

_____ Dollars

To THE PEOPLES BANK
HOUMA, LA.

The People's Bank was built on Houma's Main Street and opened in October 1896. It started with a capital outlay of $15,000. By 1900, the amount had increased to $50,000. Locally owned by many Terrebonne citizens, the facility offered local state and national financial services. The bank prospered and so did the local economy until 1927, when the "mosaic disease" destroyed the area's sugar cane crop. Most of the bank's capital had been advanced to the planters using the crop as collateral. The loans could not be paid and the bank failed. The building, then located at Main and Grinage Streets, was sold to the city and became city hall, housing the mayor's office and related services. Shown in the picture from left to right are Gabriel Montegut, Alphonse Dupont, Louis Carrane, and Julius Blum. (Courtesy of Meredith Wright.)

A landmark store in downtown Houma for many years, The Leader was located in a brick structure built in 1906. It was occupied first by Alex P. Haddad, who operated a ladies' and men's clothing store. In 1909, the business was bought by The Leader chain, which sold the same type of merchandise. The store was managed by the brothers Maurice and Julien Joseph. (Courtesy of TPCG.)

Houma's oldest continuously operating retail store was started in 1856 and did not close until 2003. It began as a bakery by French immigrant Jean Marie Dupont. Two of his sons, Albert M. and Joseph C., succeeded their father and expanded the business to include all the necessities of life. Its prime location at the corner of Main Street and U.S. Highway 90 made it convenient for customers near and far. (Courtesy of TPCG.)

Quality Furniture House, located at the corner of Main and Levron Streets, provided fine furnishings and appliances for area homes. Housed in a brick building, constructed especially for this business in 1945, the Lucas Marcello family provided spacious showrooms featuring a large selection. Brothers Ray and Curtis Marcello operated the store. (Courtesy of the Cobb collection.)

Built in 1895, the A.F. Davidson store sold everything from hardware to baby cribs, including groceries and coffins. The building housed the original location of the Bank of Houma. It was located at the corner of Main and Roussell Streets. (Courtesy of TPCG.)

The Sam Ferber Clothing Store was originally located in Lake Charles, Louisiana, from the turn of the century until Mr. Ferber's death in 1928. His wife, Augusta, and three children, Dora, Leo, and Nathan, then moved to Houma in 1933. Leo and Dora opened a ladies ready-to-wear store, which they named Palais Royale. It was located on Houma's Main Street. The photo shows Sam on the left and son Nathan on the far right. (Courtesy of the Cobb collection.)

Nathan Ferber, on the left, is shown ready to greet customers into his new Man's Shop in 1939. He offered a complete selection of men's wear next door to Palais Royale. The Ferber family businesses thrived through the 1980s, when they were sold. They were a very civic-minded family and quite charitable. Dora and Nathan each established foundations to continue their charitable activities. (Courtesy of the Cobb collection.)

William Cenac, on the far right, is shown standing in the rear of his oyster shop. As the 20th century began, Bayou Terrebonne in downtown Houma was the main means of transportation. The two-story brick building housed the Bank of Houma on the first floor and offices including the telephone exchange on the second floor. In the rear is a two-story water tower or cistern. Later, the Oyster Packing shop was demolished and the People's Bank built a brick building on the site. Both buildings still stand today. (Courtesy of Donald Cenac.)

Terrebonne Parish was the home of hundreds of acres of sugar cane production for many years. Mules and horses provided the method of gathering the crop. Cane was cut by hand in the field and gathered in wagons for the trip to the factory. Once there, the process of turning cane stalks into sugar began. This photo is from Residence Plantation, which was located on the banks of Bayou Terrebonne below Houma. (Courtesy of Wilson and Wanda Gaidry.)

Presquille Plantation, owned by the Gueno Family, was located south of Houma, where Bayou Terrebonne forked to form Bayou Little Caillou. The sugar house contained the machinery which pressed the juice from the cane stalks and converted it into molasses. The molasses was placed in wooden barrels and shipped by steamboat for further processing into sugar. (Courtesy of the Cobb collection.)

Before the turn of the 20th century, Houma was quickly becoming established as the oyster capital of North America. Oyster shuckers and Management of the People's Fish and Oyster Co. stand around their huge pile of oyster shells. The plant is in the background. Oysters, once removed from their shells, were placed in hermetically sealed cans, iced, and shipped to market by rail cars. (Courtesy of the Cobb collection.)

Shrimp drying was introduced to Terrebonne by Lee Yeun of Canton, China, in 1873. Ice was not available to preserve the catch, so large platforms such as this were built from native cypress and were located in the lakes and bays off the coast. Homes for the workers completed the operation. Supplies were brought from the mainland by boat and the dried shrimp product was returned to be packed and shipped to market. (Courtesy of the Allen J. Ellender Archives, Ellender Memorial Library, Nicholls State University, Thibodaux, Louisiana.)

As ice became available to help preserve the catch, the shrimp drying moved inland to more protected locations. The Lester Dubois family operated their drying operation on lower Bayou Little Caillou, one of the many waterways in this area. The fresh shrimp were boiled in vats of salted water and spread in the sun to dry. Later, the shells and shrimp heads were removed. At night, or in inclement weather, the shrimp were protected by tarpaulins. (Courtesy of the Cobb collection.)

Blum and Bergeron began packing and shipping dried shrimp from Houma in 1910. Most of it was packed in wooden barrels, each holding 210 pounds of dried shrimp. This shipment was packed for export to mainland China in 1925. Shown from left to right are an unidentified warehouseman, and owners Shelly J. Bergeron, Xavier H. St. Martin, and Leopold Blum. (Courtesy of Blum and Bergeron.)

The steamboat *Houma* and its sister ship *Terrebonne* brought merchandise and passengers to and from New Orleans on a regular schedule. The boats were owned by Capt. Felix Garcie and his first cousin, Capt. Millard Bradford. Their route followed Bayou Terrebonne to Canal Belanger, then to Lake Salvador, into the locks at Westwego, and then into the Mississippi River at New Orleans. Their dock was at the foot of Canal Street. (Courtesy Wilson of and Wanda Gaidry.)

Blum and Bergeron constructed their Main Street packing plant in 1921. They shared the area with oyster, fish, and fur packers in what were then the outer limits of Houma's Main Street business district. Shelley J. Bergeron (left) and Leopold Blum (right) are shown in their office. The photo was taken in 1940, shortly before Bergeron's death. (Courtesy of Blum and Bergeron.)

Here is the warehouse area of Blum and Bergeron Dried Shrimp packing plant on Houma's Main Street in 1940. Over one million pounds of dried shrimp annually were shipped by boat and rail from this location. The dried seafood was packed in wooden barrels for export or 5-10–pound paper bags in 100-pound bales for domestic use. Shown from left to right are Warehouseman Alphonse Louviere, Robert Bergeron, Morris Bergeron, and "King Cole" Tanner. (Courtesy of Blum and Bergeron.)

Shrimp canning started in Terrebonne Parish in the 1920s. The Alphonse Authement family members were pioneers in the industry. Their canning operation became flooded when Hurricane Carla hit the area in September of 1961. Like so many families in the area, as soon as the water receded, they cleaned up and restored their homes and businesses. (Courtesy of the A.P. "Tenner" Cenac Family.)

The Cure d'ars Catholic Mission Chapel was located on lower Grand Caillou, below Dulac, and served the residents of that area for many years. It faced the road, which is completely under water as the result of Hurricane Carla. The chapel escaped the flood, as it was built on pilings. (Courtesy of the A.P. "Tenner" Cenac Family.)

The Sidney Roddy barber shop and home in downtown Houma was located on Verret, between Gabasse and Barrow Streets. It was common for business owners to locate their homes either next door or on the second floor. This 1911 photo shows the hitching post in front for horses that traveled the unpaved street. The Roddy children from left to right are Nolan, Gordon, and May. Bernice is pictured next to her father. (Courtesy of the Gordon Roddy Family.)

One of the early Main Street general merchandise stores was built in 1870 by Mrs. John Milton Williams (nee Seraphine Theriot). Her father was Michel Eloie Theriot, the first white settler on Bayou Dularge. The store had a lively trade, as it was located near Main and Gabasse Streets in a newly developed suburb of the Houma village. In 1893, the property and all of the merchandise was sold to Columbus Roddy. Columbus sold to William Roddy in 1895, the year this photo was taken. Pictured standing is William. Pete Roddy is sitting. (Courtesy of the Gordon Roddy family.)

What started as a desire to arrange flowers evolved into Wurzlow Florists by Felicie Wurzlow. With the backing of her brothers, they built their shop on Goode Street in the heart of Houma in 1935. Conveniently located near St. Francis de Sales Catholic Church, Terrebonne High School, the parish court house, and the First Methodist Church, the shop enjoyed a lively business. Its home atmosphere and antique décor contributed to becoming the meeting place for all who had an interest in beauty. In 1938, Felicie married Jake Walker and turned the shop over to her sister, Olga. Olga's friends considered it a privilege to help in arranging the shop's offerings. Many gave from their own gardens. In 1947, Olga was joined by longtime family servant Eliza "Sister" Theriot. It was a common occurrence to see "Sister" snipping "fixings" from neighbors' flower gardens. This photo shows Olga about the time she became involved in the florist shop. (Courtesy of Barbara Wurzlow Picard.)

Ada Duthu Mey started her flower business in 1934 from her home on Southdown Plantation. Known for her beautiful garden and green thumb, she began making floral arrangements for friends and neighbors. In June 1938, she opened her flower shop on Main Street in downtown Houma. Her children, Bertha and Harry Jr., worked with her. Harry Jr. and Bertha purchased the business from their mother in 1943. In 1966, Harry Jr. purchased Bertha's share. The shop is now operated by Ada's grandson, Harry Mey III, and continues to provide floral arrangements to the people of this area. (Courtesy of the Harry A. Mey Sr. family.)

Residence Plantation got its name as being the home of Robert Ruffin Barrow Sr., who at one time owned many sugar plantations in Terrebonne Parish. Wilson Gaidry Sr. acquired Residence and started a dairy in 1909. This was the same year a hurricane drove many families to Houma from the low-lying areas. They contributed to Houma's demand for milk. In 1925, upon his father's death, W.J. "Piggy" Gaidry Jr. operated the business until it closed in 1965. Gaidry Sr. is shown here in his mule-driven delivery wagon. Later, Aurelie Ledet delivered from the company truck. Other dairies included Southdown, Dixie, Model, and Henderson. (Courtesy of Wilson and Wanda Gaidry.)

The largest gas well in the world at that time began production in 1917. Located below Montegut, in what eventually became known as the Lirette Field, this was the beginning of the "petro economy," which still fuels Houma's wealth. The Terrebonne Gas Co. piped and supplied fuel to Houma and six area sugar refineries until 1930, when salt water incursion curtailed production. (Courtesy of the Cobb collection.)

During the 1930s, the Texas Oil Company, later Texaco, established production of oil and gas in Terrebonne Parish. A lot of their operations were located in the lakes and bays in the coastal areas. The tugboat *Houma* was a part of the fleet that serviced those operations. Texaco became the largest employer. Their operations were housed in a large office building with a slip and docks in Houma, a short distance from the Intracoastal Canal. (Courtesy of TPCG.)

"Philip Morris" came to Houma in 1950, not as a then-popular cigarette, but as a furniture store. In the late 1940s, Philip Solsolsky and Morris Itzkovitch became partners in a retail furniture establishment. Solsolsky-Itzkovitch just did not seem appealing as a name for the new venture. By using their two first names, a possible conflict with the cigarette company seemed likely, but the cigarette company welcomed the new venture and sent their trademark advertiser "Johnnie" to Houma to highlight the store's opening. Johnnie, the hotel "Call Boy," was shown in the cigarette ad walking through a crowded lobby announcing "Call for Philip Morris." He is shown shaking hands with store manager Jack G. Shearer. The unidentified onlooker is a representative of the cigarette manufacturer. The store was located in a two-story building on Barrow Street near Main Street. (Courtesy of Ivy J. Smith.)

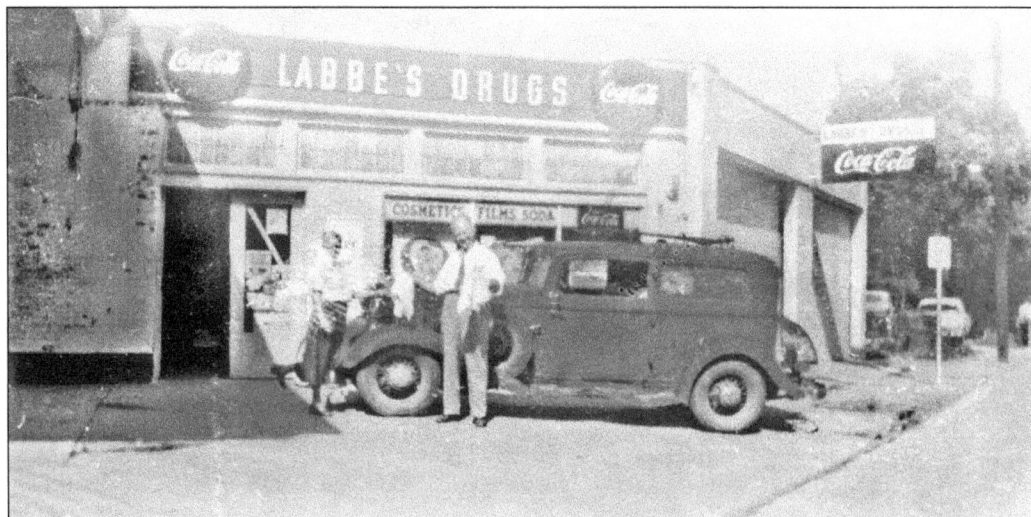

Labbe's Drug Store, at the corner of Goode and Belanger Streets, opened in 1930. It was owned and operated by Waldo J. Labbe Sr., a third-generation pharmacist and native of St. Martinville, Louisiana. Mrs. Labbe had a sandwich and homemade ice cream counter at this popular gathering place for the courthouse crowd and students from Terrebonne High School. The pharmacy operated until Labbe's retirement in 1971. (Courtesy of the Allen J. Ellender Archives, Ellender Memorial Library, Nicholls State University, Thibodaux, Louisiana.)

Six

MEMORIES

This is Main Street at the intersection of Lafayette Street as it appeared in 1910 looking east. The oak trees marking the courthouse are in the far distance. The tower on the left marks the Knights of Pythias Castle Hall, a fraternal lodge meeting place. The local newspaper, *Houma Times*, Dried Shrimp Packer Blum and Bergeron, the Ladies Parlor, and the Pelican Restaurant complete the north side. On the south side is the newly constructed brick Bonvillain building at the intersection of Main and Court (later Belanger Street). Behind the parked horse and buggy is the office of Charles Menville M.D. and the Louis Menville Pharmacy. The Hotel Durant and Lewald's Clothing Store complete the block. (Courtesy of the Cobb collection.)

Main Street, looking west near the corner of Roussell Street in July of 1907, is an unpaved dirt thoroughfare with a wooden sidewalk. The banner advertises a sale at the Houma Bargain store. The Houma city hall is next to Berger Bros. Livery and Feed and the tower identifying the opera house is on the horizon. Electricity was generated and sold by the Houma Ice Co. Telephone service was provided by the Cumberland Telephone and Telegraph Co. (Courtesy of the Cobb collection.)

Houma citizens always turned out in large numbers for a parade. This is a 1936 Mardi Gras parade, complete with mule drawn float. "T-Con" Duplantis was responsible for the local group that contracted the floats and were the riders. "Throw me something" cries from the onlookers resulted in glass beads imported from Czechoslovakia being thrown to the crowd. The parade is headed west, just past the corner of Main and Church Streets. (Courtesy of Wilson and Wanda Guidry.)

This early motor car was brought to Houma by the Berger Bros. Livery and Feed. It had a hard time navigating the dirt streets and roads when they turned to mud. The vehicle was available to rent for those brave enough to do so. It was purchased to show the public that a horse and buggy was the most dependable method of transportation. (Courtesy of the Cobb collection.)

By the 1950s, the horse and buggy, along with the livery stables, were gone. The motor car was king of the road and Houma had many dealerships. Liberty Auto Sales, located on Barrow Street, was owned and operated by I.W. "Bud" Sharp. (Courtesy of Ivy Smith.)

This is the home of Mrs. Caliste Bourgeois, located at the corner of Verret and Grinage Streets. Born in France in 1856, the only daughter of Jean Monthieu and Bertrand de Soupsole, Eleanore Monthieu arrived in Morgan City with her mother to join her father when she was 12 years of age. Shortly after that, they made their home in Houma. Eleanore later married Caliste Bourgeois. By 1891, she was a widow with six children. When she died in 1937, she was Houma's oldest native of France. (Courtesy of Donald Cenac.)

The stately home of Lucius Fane Suthon stood on Main Street. It is now the site of the original Terrebonne General Hospital. Only the oak trees have survived. Suthon was a native of Scotland and a graduate of Edinburgh University. He settled in Terrebonne in 1875, where he practiced law. As a land owner and businessman, he helped organize the Bank of Houma. He became president of the Houma Fish and Oyster Co. and the general manager of the sugar plantations owned by the estate of H.C. Minor. He also owned Honduras Plantation and developed the subdivision in N. Houma with streets bearing his name: Lucius, Fane, and Suthon. (Courtesy of the L.F. Suthon Family.)

114

This beautiful turn-of-the-century home of Frank Wurzlow Sr. was the first residence to be built on Wilson Avenue in North Houma. The street was named for Harry L. Wilson, the engineer that operated the ice and electricity manufacturing facilities, which were owned by Dr. L.H. Jastremski, developer of the subdivision. Frank Wurzlow was an enterprising Houma native. He established one of the first movie theaters, The Wonderland, managed the Commercial Hotel, and had an unshakeable belief as early as 1906 that there was oil and gas under the "Good Earth." He lived long enough to have this confirmed and to prosper from mineral leases. (Courtesy of Barbara Wurzlow Picard.)

The Houma Volunteer Fire Company turned out in uniform during the 1920s for this Main Street group photo. In the foreground is the drain cover, as the street was then unpaved. Sitting at the wheel of the fire truck is Albert Doiron. The others are unidentified. On the right are the Grand Theatre, the Blahut Store, and the A.F. Davidson building at the corner of Main and Roussell Streets. On the left are Porche Bros. Automobile dealership and the Jaccuzzo building. (Courtesy of Peggy T. Wurzlow.)

One of Houma's earliest buildings was located at the corner of Roussell and Court (Belanger) Streets. This long, one-story shotgun style structure was known as Breaux's Beanery. Pierre Breaux operated a room and board establishment and served mostly beans and rice. Later, the property was owned by Sidney Fabregas. He and his wife Sue made their home in this historic structure. Sidney operated a livery stable in the backyard barn facing Court Street. (Courtesy of the Allen J. Ellender Archives, Ellender Memorial Library, Nicholls State University, Thibodaux, Louisiana.)

This large home was one of the first to be built on Houma's Main Street, corner of Gabasse. In 1859, Mrs. John Milton Williams, daughter of Terrebonne Pioneer Michel Eloi Theriot, built the house and raised her family. She sold to Jean M. Dupont in 1895. His son, Albert, had it raised and enlarged to accommodate his family. His brother, Joseph C., owned his home on the opposite corner across Gabasse Street. (Courtesy of the Cobb collection.)

This is Timbalier Bay Lighthouse as it appeared in 1911, complete with bathing beauties. From left to right are the following: (front row) Eva Bazet Zelenka, unidentified, and Clara Mildred Smith; (back row) Thelma Zelenka, May B. Lester Dupont, Victoire Marmande Breaux, Mr. Grey (lighthouse keeper), and three unidentified. Note the large cistern for fresh water and the keeper's home in the rear. (Courtesy of the Cobb collection.)

The Timbalier Bay Lighthouse was completed in 1917. The first coast light was built in 1856 and was destroyed by a hurricane in 1867. The replacement came in 1875 and lasted until erosion toppled it in 1894. Timbalier is an important entrance point from the Gulf of Mexico to the bays, lakes, and bayous of Terrebonne Parish. (Courtesy of Connie Townsend.)

This was Main Street looking east from the intersection of Barataria as it appeared in the 1930s. On the right is Ane Brothers General Merchandise, built on the recently filled Barataria Canal. On the left is Elster's Clothing Store. Opened in 1911 by Joseph Elster, the business featured ladies' and men's ready-to-wear. After Joseph's death, the business was operated by his son, Marty, and his wife, Frances, until Marty's death in the late 1980s. (Courtesy TPCG.)

F.W. Woolworth opened this downtown store in a new building constructed for them in 1940. Space was made for the lunch counter installed in the main merchandise area 25 years later. It quickly became a popular place for Woolworth customers to patronize as well as neighboring merchants and Main Street shoppers to assemble. Sandwiches, beverages, and lunches were regular features. Shown sitting is Selma Geiger. (Courtesy of Emanuel and Selma Geiger.)

118

Downtown Houma's Commercial Bar was separated from the Commercial Hotel by an enclosed alleyway. The alleyway at various times housed a shoe shine stand and was the original location of Universal Tailors. The main building dates from 1872 and was the home of Francois Gouaux's pharmacy. It later housed various retail merchandise and grocery businesses. Today, it is the office of Appellate Court Judge John Pettigrew. This photo is from the 1950s. (Courtesy of the Allen J. Ellender Archives, Ellender Memorial Library, Nicholls State University, Thibodaux, Louisiana.)

The Bazet Hotel was a familiar landmark on Church Street in downtown Houma. It was built after the Main Street fire of December 29, 1887 destroyed the original hotel and related Bazet holdings. Owned and operated by Bernard F. Bazet and his wife, the former Ernestine Theriot, the hotel quickly gained a reputation for her cooking and hospitality. It remained an operating hotel until the mid-1930s. It was demolished in 1951. (Courtesy of the Allen J. Ellender Archives. Ellender, Memorial Library, Nicholls State University, Thibodaux, Louisiana.)

This Acadian-style home on Barrow Street near Main, was originally built in the 1850s to be a boarding school. It became the home of Henry Franklin Belanger and his wife, the former Henrietta Boutelace, in 1864. H.F. Belanger operated a Main Street pharmacy starting in 1857. His son and daughter both became pharmacists. Jim and Edith Belanger operated the drug store until Jim's death in the late 1940s. Their home was torn down in 1950. (Courtesy of the Allen J. Ellender Archives, Ellender Memorial Library, Nicholls State University, Thibodaux, Louisiana.)

This scene was very common on Bayou Terrebonne in downtown Houma until the waterway was declared non-navigable by an act of Congress in the early 1950s. *The Florence J.* was part of a fleet owned by the Leon H. Jastremski Family. It was used in their shrimping operations, which included a large drying operation, a canning plant, and an ice manufacturing business. (Courtesy of the Cobb collection.)

Seven

BRIDGING THE PAST

On December 16, 1935, a remarkable event occurred when the Bridge at Nine Mile Point above New Orleans was dedicated. Built at the height of the Great Depression under the administrations of governors Huey P. Long and Oscar K. Allen, the structure quickly became known as the "Huey P." The combination railroad and highway bridge over the mighty Mississippi cost $13,000,000. Prior to completion, rail cars were barged and vehicles were ferried. Many feared the structure would collapse when put into use. A prominent member of the Houma delegation riding in the motorcade to the dedication insisted on being in the last car—he was not taking any chances and felt safer being the last car to cross. With the advent of television in 1950, many feared the iron superstructure would make television reception in Houma impossible. This was proved wrong when a fearless radio dealer bought a set, installed a 60-foot- high antenna, and produced a watchable picture in his Main Street display window. (Courtesy of the Cobb collection.)

The corner of Main Street and Church Street was the site of one of downtown Houma's street paving projects on April 21, 1936. The whole downtown area was eventually paved using federal WPA funds. This program was part of the federal effort to infuse a massive amount of dollars into the local economy during the 1930s depression. From left to right, are Harvey Hebert, T. Baker Smith (city engineer), Gaston Theriot (Public Works Administration engineer), Leopold Blum (alderman), Harry Hellier, (mayor pro tem), William Cenac (alderman), David J. Olivier (alderman), William Drott (assistant city clerk), and Dreux Angers (city clerk). Dumping the first batch of cement is Ald. Louis C. LeBlanc. (Courtesy of the Cobb collection.)

Here is Houma's Main Street looking west from the corner of Church Street shortly before the 1936 cement paving project. Clam shells and subsurface drainage kept the downtown streets passable during the frequent rains. A close look will reveal the three downtown hotels of the era: Rhodes, Commercial, and City. The Knights of Pythias Lodge Hall Tower, a Main Street landmark, can be seen in the background on the right. (Courtesy of TPCG.)

This is Houma's Main Street looking west from the corner of Church Street in 1940 upon completion of the downtown street paving project. The subsurface storm drains previously installed greatly assisted rain runoff from the cement paving. The new surface required mechanical street sweepers, which the city acquired. (Courtesy of the Allen J. Ellender Archives, Ellender Memorial Library, Nicholls State University, Thibodaux, Louisiana.)

Popularly known as the "old rooster" because of the weather vain on the cupola, this edifice was located on Church Street between School and Verret Streets. It became a school house in 1898 and Terrebonne High School in 1900. This was the first public high school in Houma. (Courtesy of TPCG.)

By 1918, the Terrebonne Parish school system acquired the use of the entire block between School, Verret, Goode, and Church Streets. This three-story brick building served as high school classrooms and school board offices. By 1940, the high school was moved to its present location on Main Street and Junior High classes were housed in this location. (Courtesy of TPCG.)

124

Occupying the entire block encircled by Barrow, Academy, Lee and Bond Streets, the St. Francis de Sales Academy was originally built in 1850 as a private school known as the "Houma Academy." It was acquired by the Marianite Sisters in 1870 and is the forerunner of Vandebilt Catholic High School. (Courtesy of the Allen J. Ellender Archives, Ellender Memorial Library, Nicholls State University, Thibodaux, Louisiana.)

The Catholic Parish of St. Frances de Sales came to downtown Houma in 1847, hence the Church Street name. This church building was torn down to make way for the present church structure, completed in 1936. The property was acquired as part of the Belanger-Grinage grant to the police jury. It took an act of the state legislature on April 25, 1936 to finally affirm the church's ownership. (Courtesy of TPCG.)

St. Francis de Sales school and church were completed in 1936, largely through the efforts of its pastor, Rev. Father August Vanderbilt. Upon his death on April 7, 1938, he left his estate to the church. This contributed significantly to retiring the debt incurred to build the imposing edifice. In 1964, the interior was given its first renovation. The architectural integrity was not disturbed, but merely enhanced. In 1977, the Diocese of Houma-Thibodaux was established and St. Francis was chosen to be the cathedral. Major interior and exterior renovations were undertaken to further enhance the architectural features. Exterior lighting accents the site, making it the centerpiece along with the courthouse square of today's downtown Houma area. (Courtesy of the Cobb collection.)

This is St. Matthew's Episcopal Church as it looked in 1858. Uncommon at that time, it was a brick building with a single steeple and large windows. It was located on the same property that today's church is standing. It was erected at a cost of $7,050 and was completed on July 20, 1858. At that time, the minister's salary was determined by the rental of the pews. The rector was Leonidas Polk, the first Episcopal Bishop of Louisiana, who held services in the Terrebonne Parish Courthouse and in private homes prior to the building of this church. A double disaster hit St. Matthew's during the period of 1888 and 1890. The rectory burned, and the church building was declared unsafe, requiring its demolition. (Courtesy of Roland J. Champagne.)

St. Matthew's Episcopal Church is a prominent landmark on tree-shaded Barrow Street in downtown Houma. It is situated on property donated by Robert Ruffin Barrow. Construction of the present building was completed in 1892. The addition of the parish hall, to the right of and adjoining the church, was added in 1913. In 1989, St. Matthew's was listed on the National Register of Historic Places. All of the oak trees except the one nearest Main Street are over 125 years old. They became members of the Live Oak Society and are named Abraham, Sarah, Isaac, Jacob-Israel, and Joseph. Another tree which came with newly acquired property will be named "The Prodigal Son." (Courtesy of Roland J. Champagne.)

Terrebonne Parish at one time abounded with virgin cypress in its swamps. By the 1920s, they had been cut and processed into lumber, marketed as "the wood eternal." Only the second growth remains, along with the many canals cut through the swamp area to gather and transport the logs to the saw mills. A lot has been harvested from this area: lumber, seafood, fur, oil, natural gas, sugar cane, fruits, vegetables, and even Easter lilies. Like the new growth found in our swamps, we will survive and have a bright future. (Courtesy of the Cobb collection.)

www.ingramcontent.com/pod-product-compliance
Lightning Source LLC
Chambersburg PA
CBHW050635110426

42813CB00007B/1820